# Journey of Faith

Nora Pinter

ISBN 979-8-88540-966-7 (paperback)
ISBN 979-8-88540-967-4 (digital)

Copyright © 2023 by Nora Pinter

All rights reserved. No part of this publication may be reproduced, distributed, or transmitted in any form or by any means, including photocopying, recording, or other electronic or mechanical methods without the prior written permission of the publisher. For permission requests, solicit the publisher via the address below.

Christian Faith Publishing
832 Park Avenue
Meadville, PA 16335
www.christianfaithpublishing.com

Printed in the United States of America

# Preface

Saigon, Vietnam, March 1966. Wade and Ruth Kincaid had arrived at the airport in Saigon. This had been quite a journey, and as they had winged their way over the blue Pacific, it seemed as though they were part of a miracle. This had been a takeoff into the unknown for them. Pop and Mom, as they will become affectionately known to the servicemen, are sixty-five and sixty-four, respectively.

Their thoughts went back over the years of evangelizing and pastoring. They had been comfortably settled in a little farming community in Eastern Washington, about sixty-five miles south of Spokane, Washington, pastoring an independent church and living in the parsonage just across the street from the church. The church is old and had curved wooden benches for pews and beautiful stained-glass windows. There is a high steeple with a bell that Pop would ring every Sunday morning and evening and Wednesday evening before services. They seemed content to be at this stage in their lives with family grown and grandchildren to bless them until one day, in 1964, Pop received an invitation to go to Japan on an evangelistic trip which was only to be for about two weeks. He knew that financially, they could not possibly attempt to go on such a trip, but he decided to discuss this with Mom and see what she had to say. Of course, Mom said, "I think that will be fine, I can take care of the services here." Much to their surprise, funds began to come to them from unexpected sources to make it possible that both would be able to make the trip. They lingered in their thoughts over the part of this ten-day crusade in Japan. At least it was to be a ten-day crusade, but they had actually stayed for two months evangelizing.

Japan. In Tokyo, September 1964, they were involved in meetings morning and afternoon. Pop spoke to a gathering of college students also. The next stop was Nagoya, Japan, where they were in meetings for three weeks. They enjoyed the fast train trip from Tokyo to Nagoya but traveling by taxi in Tokyo was quite an experience. Taxis drive on the opposite side of the road than in the US and don't have lanes marked on many streets. They visited Nishinomiya, sister city of Spokane, Washington, and the mayor of Nishinomiya came to welcome them to the city and to take them on a tour.

Pop spoke through an interpreter which was a new experience for him. They so appreciated the wonderful hospitality and being able to visit places of interest. All in all, this was a very rewarding and inspiring trip for them. It may have been the Lord's way of preparing their hearts for the next big adventure. They were so blessed to see many lives changed by the power of the Word preached in those few weeks.

Now their path was leading to Vietnam in 1966 and the establishment of the first Christian Servicemen's Center in Saigon during the war years.

*God was preparing our hearts for what was to follow.*

Our Japan experience helped us accept the surprising challenge that came about a year later. I have found that God doesn't bring us to a new place of service without having prepared us through what we have experienced in the past. When David was to meet Goliath, he had already met the lion and the bear.

We received a letter from Rev. Eddie Karnes of World Harvesters. He had visited Vietnam, saw there was no place for American servicemen to go during off-duty hours (except to the bars), and told us of the need for a servicemen's center. The boys needed a home away from home. Would we consider going?

"I know how to make a home, and that is what these young fellows need desperately," Ruth declared. "Let's go!"

We were told that we must go from church to church and raise the money for our return trip in case we had to come home in a hurry. We itinerated only one month. Feeling the urge to get to Saigon as soon as possible, we decided to use our own funds. This saved much time in getting to Vietnam.

# A New Adventure

We were going into the unknown, and we learned as we went along, always grateful for any knowledgeable help that was offered. One suggestion was that we should make several overnight stops on the way to prevent our becoming too weary. I was sixty-five and Ruth was sixty-four, a bit past the prime of youth. The Vietnamese consulate in Washington would only give us a thirty-day visa and told us that it might take several months to get one from Saigon. We decided to go on with the thirty-day visa and try getting the other after getting to Vietnam.

We left Los Angeles, California, in March of 1966, with overnight stops in Hawaii, Japan, Philippines, and Hong Kong, arriving in Vietnam just as the sun was setting on March 15, 1966. We had lots of luggage and felt worn in body. As we waited to get through customs, I decided that moving our luggage along inch by inch was not the practical thing to do. We would wait until the others got through then take them all at once.

A Vietnamese officer stepped to the railing, picked up part of our luggage, and said, "Follow me." We gathered our things and followed him out. We were handed our papers all ready to go in no time at all. It was a strange and wonderful thing.

I had been told to get in touch with the Christian and Missionary Alliance Rest Home for missionaries. We planned to stay a day or two until we could get a place of our own.

As I went to look for a telephone, a Vietnamese policeman appeared. When he was within six feet of me, he asked, "Are you a Christian?" What an odd thing for a stranger to ask!

I replied, "Yes, I am."

"Me too," he said and crossed himself.

I figured he was a friend and could speak English, so I asked him about a telephone. "Come into my office," he invited. "Sit down and I will make the call for you." And he did. We were soon on our way.

# Frustration

Everything seemed to be continually moving in Vietnam due to the war activities. We found that renting a place, however small, was next to impossible. Patience and faith were sorely tried.

In time, we did get settled only to have the owner come the very next day and say that something had happened in the family, and they had to have the place! However, God eventually provided.

# Reaching Out

It didn't take long for the fact that we were there to be known abroad in the land. And they began coming. Some of our boys wanted to know about the Lord and how to serve Him in such a situation as Nam. We did our best to take them to the Word of God for their answers. The Gospel of John was especially helpful to us personally and we clung to Hebrews 13:8, "Jesus Christ the same yesterday, today, and forever."

Our men appreciated a place where they could come and sit down in the quiet of a home-like atmosphere and maybe talk about a problem that had come into their lives. We became known as Mom and Pop to all of them. They unburdened their hearts. We gave advice and prayed with them.

# House Church

Soon we were having services in our home. Men were glad to come to nondenominational meetings. We held up the Lord Jesus Christ as the One who loved them and had redeemed them by his death on Calvary. Most of them were anxious to make sure of their personal standing with the Lord. We stressed that we can *know* our relationship with Him.

How they did enjoy singing the old-time hymns! Some chaplains attended. Other young fellows had quite a knowledge of the Bible and there were some good preachers among them. Others led song service or took part in whatever way they could. They entered right into it. I think we all tried to put into practice the words on the sign at the Nha Trang Chapel:

> Don't count the days.
> Make the days count.

Now my best recounting of life in Saigon is from letters we sent out to family, friends, and contributors.

# UNDATED LETTER

We had not been in Saigon very long when I was asked to see a serviceman in Pleiku about four hundred miles up the country from Saigon at the request of his son in Germany. I did not have travel orders yet but the men at the air base in Saigon let me on a plane. However, they warned me that I might have trouble getting back. I could not find the man when I got to Pleiku so I had to stay overnight at Camp Enari which was about eight miles from Pleiku. The next morning, I did find the man and was able to visit with him. To return to Saigon, I was manifested on an army plane called the Caribou. The plane stopped at Nha Trang, and everyone got off the plane there. The Air Force men wouldn't let me get back on because I didn't have travel orders. Mr. Morgan, who ran a servicemen's center there, took me over to the army base. There I was told there would be no flight out until the next day at 6:00 p.m., so I had to stay over another night. I had a good visit with the Morgan's and got home safe. I know Mom was very concerned when I did not return the same night.

The night before last, the artillery fire was so heavy that one could hardly sleep, the mortars that the VC sent slamming into the city was anything but soothing to the nerves.

Last Thursday, I went by helicopter to Long Binh to visit in the big hospital. I took 110 booklets, "Here's How," and gave them all out before I had visited all the wards. It was the reward of a lifetime just to get to visit with the men and talk to them about the Lord and have prayer with them. They seemed to appreciate having me come down as they seldom ever see a civilian.

One coming here must be prepared to face many discouraging things. The language barrier is a difficult thing. One has to learn that when the Vietnamese say yes, he may mean no, and the other way around. So confusing.

## April 6, 1966

There was a demonstration here Monday night, so they have imposed a curfew from 9:00 p.m. to 5:00 a.m. We got out this morning and got our ID cards. Now we can buy at the army commissary. This will be a great help to us as well as a saving in money.

## May 8, 1966

We had a well with a manually operated electric pump that fills a fifty-gallon oil drum on top of the house. This supplied the bathroom. We had five clay urns which held about fifty gallons each. We kept them full. In one, we had a filter that siphoned out about one quart every two hours. This we boiled and strained through cotton before we drank. When we first came, we could pump the well dry in three or four minutes. But we didn't have to worry about that for the next four months, as this was the monsoon season—how it rains here! We had the privilege of buying at the army commissary, so we were able to get good food to eat. We could even buy fresh milk from California. Of course, it was canned but not condensed. We sent a Vietnamese girl to the local market for bananas and papaya, as she could buy them for about half of what we could. We washed our clothes in a big pan. I washed the sheets, and Mom washed the other things. Drying would be a problem from now on. The breezeway between our living room and kitchen got water all over it. The Lord had been so good to us. He had given us some very fine Vietnamese friends. The electricity was off from 3:00 p.m. until 9:00 p.m. We went to town this afternoon and got home about 6:00 p.m. A young Vietnamese man had just come to see us. We told him that we didn't have any lights. He started to go after some candles for us. Just then, his brother came with four candles. He had read in the paper that the lights would be off, so he brought candles to us. He later brought us a little kerosene lamp. These were some of the good things that came to us here.

# June 13, 1966

(Mom writing)

Pop went over to the Special Services Department this morning; it was some walk. But then he killed two birds with one stone—or walk—as he always met soldiers and he gave out tracts and talks to them. You know, when we first came here, it seemed easier for me than Pop to give out tracts, but now he does fine. Sometimes he talked as long as fifteen or twenty minutes, and the servicemen were usually anxious to visit.

# June 29, 1966

To give you a little idea of a day's schedule, yesterday I got up at 6:00 a.m. We ate breakfast at 7:15 a.m. and then did our daily devotions. We got ready and went to Chalon to the commissary. We got there by taxi at 9:00 a.m. It didn't open until 10:00 a.m., so we used that time to visit one of the chaplains and then give out tracts. We were able to give out all the tracts we had with us before the store opened. While we were getting our groceries, we found a man we knew, so we asked if he would take us home, and he did. We got home just at noon. As it was pouring down all afternoon, we spent some time writing letters.

We were able to go out later in the afternoon and give out tracts and be back home at 4:00 p.m. We had two servicemen coming for supper.

So far, as we were able to find out, we were the only ones giving out tracts to the servicemen in Saigon. With over three hundred thousand men over here, think of the job we had. I really thought this was one of the greatest ministries we had ever been privileged to have.

# July 7, 1966

(Mom writing to one of her grandchildren)

There were so many children all around us, but none of them could understand what you would say to them. We didn't have our dear little grandchildren here, so we had to love the little Vietnamese boys and girls.

I went to town this morning and I rode in a cyclo-may, a three-wheeled bicycle with a seat in front. I got home from town about noon. John (a serviceman) was here for lunch. Then he and Qui (our Vietnamese neighbor boy) played ball, while Grandpa and I did the dishes. Grandpa and John would be leaving in a while to go down to Saigon to give out tracts.

# July 18, 1966

One of the servicemen just came in and brought Mom a nice bouquet of roses. They did have really beautiful flowers here and were not very expensive either.

It did seem that our days were so full. One big problem here was transportation. We lost a lot of time waiting for a taxi or a bus.

# August 7, 1966

We had a nice (thirty-eighth) anniversary dinner Sunday. A young serviceman took us out to dinner. He had to work on Monday so he said he would take us Sunday afternoon. It was very nice, and we did enjoy it very much.

Mom has mentioned so many times how she wishes her grandchildren could be here to wade in the water in our breezeway when it rains—and that is just about every day now. But we were very glad it rained! It gets terribly hot between showers. This again shows the wisdom of God. Though we are north of the equator, and it was the summer season, yet it was really the coolest because of the monsoon season. They told us that the rains begin to taper off in September. There is little or no rain from November to May. So these are the hot months. They told us that the average temperature here is very close to ninety with the humidity being about equal.

I saw in the Saigon paper that Dr. Bob Pierce is going to build a big orphanage that will take care of about eight hundred orphans. There were many here and there will be more. Some of the servicemen that went to work at five or six in the morning told me that they see from ten or twenty-five children sleeping in the doorways of the downtown stores, besides the many sleeping in the little parks. They shined shoes, sold papers, begged, and stole to get something to eat.

## August 16, 1966

We had sure been busy lately. More and more of the boys had been coming here. Of course, that was what we were here for, but we had to keep up our tract work also.

# September 14, 1966

Some Vietnamese ministers invited me to go to the city of Ben Hoa where they held an open-air service and gave out tracts. So we left this morning at eight o'clock and got back a little after noon. I knew this will be hard for some to believe, but I started to give out tracts in the street by the open market and soon they (Vietnamese) thronged around me until I had to hold the tracts above my head to keep them from grabbing the tracts all away from me. Then I realized that with my hands up, I would be an easy prey for the pickpockets who are always around over here, so I just had to take off and get out of their way. You sure never have that kind of trouble when giving out tracts in the States.

The other night, while we slept, someone climbed over the wall with the barbed wire on top then climbed over the high wall and down into our breezeway. They took more than twenty-five dollars' worth of groceries. They just about cleaned our refrigerator out. They took the cord and heat control for our electric frying pan. I don't know why they left the pan. They took our two-quart insulated water pitcher. We have moved our refrigerator and everything into a room where we can lock it up and have asked the landlord to screen in the breezeway or put an iron accordion grating in front of the kitchen.

Last night, one of the special forces men was here. He worked out among the tribes' people where the VC are active robbing and harassing the village people. He gave his testimony of how the Lord saved him and has kept him safe while working in such a dangerous area. Yesterday was the first time in seven months that he had been away from his post of duty. Someone had given him our address, so he had come to see us. He is a married man, just married two months before he got orders to come over here.

## September 29, 1966

Qui, our Vietnamese neighbor boy, was here. He helped us so much. He cooked rice in an open kettle 'till it is just perfect. He ran a lot of errands for us and never took any pay for it.

There was a serviceman here sleeping in the room where we have been locking things up, so we forgot to put the toaster and big fan in, and the thieves came again and got the toaster and fan and a few other things. But we are still alive and well, so that is what really counts.

# October 22, 1966

We were told today that we would not be able to buy in the commissary after the first of November. As long as the navy was in charge of this, we were all right, but the army had taken over now, and they had some strange ideas. But this didn't worry us. There were over twenty-five thousand men here that could go in and buy for us anything that we may need. It was a little more inconvenient, as we had to bother someone else to go for us.

# November 7, 1966

*I* had my first baptismal service in a foreign land yesterday. Everyone said that it was a very beautiful service.

# November 21, 1966

This afternoon, Lan, our Vietnamese neighbor and brother of Qui, his wife, and six children came over. They had everything for our noon meal. All Vietnamese dishes. The soup was very good, made of very fine noodles that were like grass with chicken on top. Then a salad and noodles, meat and shrimp rolled in rice paper and fried in deep fat. It was all very good. Our chaplain and John were here also.

## December 1966

One of our servicemen, John, had been decorating our home for us. We were able to get a Christmas tree. This was some kind of a pine, rather scrubby but we thought it was beautiful.

In the afternoon, I went to Tan Son Nhut Air Base for a Christmas party for some refugee orphan children.

# About Christmas

The Friday evening before Christmas, we invited Qui, his father and mother, Lan, his wife, and their six children, two cousins, Qui's younger brother, and a sister. John, a serviceman, was also here. Qui and Lan's father taught sculpturing at the University of Saigon, and their mother is the granddaughter of a former king. After we had refreshments, we had the Christmas story read from St. Luke. John read some in English, then Lan read it in Vietnamese so that his parents could understand it. After this, the little ones were given a present.

On Christmas Day, the only serviceman that was free to have Christmas dinner with us was Dr. Gladheart from the air base. In the afternoon, Dr. Gladheart took Mom with him to one of the orphanages where he had toys and presents to give out to the children. Mom so enjoyed this time.

# January 1967

*W*e have had our commissary privileges restored. It took a little time to get some things worked out.

*Mom Writing*

Yesterday I went to the base and started to give out tracts. I had the "Here's How" tract in which we had put a picture of Jesus and a small calendar. Very seldom a man will refuse a tract; in fact, yesterday, a man came back and asked if he could have one to send to his folks. Strange world, isn't it? A serviceman from Nha Trang had been visiting us, and he said, "You couldn't give out tracts like that in the States, you would embarrass people." How about that? Better be a little embarrassed.

When we heard a big boom in the night, we didn't ask "My, what was that?" for we know some shooting was going on. Then we heard the planes zoom out, as we were close to the base (the busiest in the world). Then late at night or early in the morning, the big helicopters came lumbering in with the wounded or the dead.

Rent was due today. That was another thing, how our needs had been met. It was only a miracle. We had paid very little rent in our life, but now we paid almost $300, and every month the Lord would supply. Praise God.

Pop was up at 5:30 a.m. to attend a breakfast for ministers and missionaries. When he got home, we went to the Third Field Hospital to visit.

# February 1967

A couple who worked in Saigon visited us. They were so pleased with what they saw that they wanted to help by sending us a big roasted turkey for our Sunday dinner. There were fourteen of us to enjoy it.

We were able to get into the hospitals which does expand our field of influence.

It really had been a miracle the way our needs have been supplied. Eddie Karnes with World Harvesters had promised to help each month with the support of this venture, but some months he hadn't sent us anything, but as we had said before, by some miracle, other money had come in for the rent, etc. When he had sent money, it was usually just $200, which is just $71 less than the rent. We believed that the Lord supplies, for if we couldn't believe this, we just as well come home now. When one is out like this, there is only one thing to do, and that is to trust the Lord. One must not panic but just rest in the faithfulness of God.

We were having what the Vietnamese call their New Year (or Tet). They shot a lot of firecrackers and had quite a celebration. One would think they wouldn't want to shoot firecrackers when they could hear the big guns night and day, but that was their way. They gave gifts at this time, the same as we do at Christmastime. They played games and did a lot of gambling. I think this went on for about one week.

We had a nice big sign-up on Truong Minh Giang Street and one here at the gate.

I must tell you what a young man said that came here last night. There had been a mix-up in his orders to return to the States, and he was so disappointed and depressed that he just didn't know what to do. He said, "I just don't know what I would have done if I hadn't been able to come here and talk with you this evening."

The man and his wife that sent the roast turkey to us also promised to put a sink in our kitchen for Mom, and the landlord was having the city water put in which will be much better.

We had been blessed to be able to have an APO address through a serviceman stationed here. His name is Richard, and last night he brought us a lot of mail.

I was sent a notice to be on jury duty in the States but I have written the sheriff to excuse me and I really don't expect that they will want me to come from so far.

We were coming into the hot season of the year now. It was plenty warm today. It was about the last of April before we began to get much rain. Everything was dry and dusty now.

We had the smallest refrigerator, but a serviceman gave us a nice big refrigerator to use. It was the size of the one we have at home or a little bigger. We had a chest-type freezer promised to us, so it looks like we will be getting fixed up a little more like home. They hooked up the city water last Saturday, for which I am very thankful. The well water was really getting bad. I didn't even like to take a shower in it. The Lord is so good to us.

Mom was thrilled the other day when a young man came in and said, "My, it is so good to be home again." He had been in the active war zone and was soon to leave for the Philippines.

Last night, a man came to us so disturbed and confused about his spiritual condition. We ministered from the Word of God and saw him leave with the peace of God in his heart.

# June 1967

We have moved to larger quarters, but the electricity supply was inadequate. Saturday evening, about time for our service to start, the power went off. Not only would we be without lights but also we would have no fans. And you just have to be here to know what that means. We have moved into an area where the electricity goes off a lot.

We had each man take a metal folding chair up to the roof of the house. We had a flat concrete roof with room to seat 150. What a service we had! Such singing you could hardly expect at this side of heaven and testimonies that would thrill your soul! A young serviceman did the preaching, and he did a good job.

We have set aside one room here where the men can pray or study in any free time. It isn't very easy to pray in the barracks.

This seemed like such a nice cool morning until I looked at the thermometer and noticed that it registered eighty-four degrees at 8:00 a.m.

We have met some on the street of Saigon who told us they had once known Christ but had left Him since coming here. We try to help them.

# July 1967

We are going to the Third Field Hospital now to see a young man who has lost his leg and has had an infection in it. From there, we went to the base for a chapel service. This had been a great day here. A young man just came in for a few minutes to see us. He had been in Japan and is now stationed someplace here in Vietnam.

# September 1967

We have been here almost eighteen months. The enemy tried to make it look as though the Christian cause is lost, and the evil forces will swallow up the church, but we have taken our orders from the Lord to go forward. We are now having regular Sunday morning and evening services. In our first Sunday night service, a young man gave his heart to the Lord.

# October 1967

We took a little vacation this week. One of the servicemen on leave volunteered to stay and look after the center while we went to Dalat for a day. Dalat is up in the mountains, a very pretty place, about a three hundred-mile trip. We wanted to visit the Jacksons who have spent about forty years in Vietnam with the Christian and Missionary Alliance. They work with the Montagnards spoken of in the book, "The Bamboo Cross."

Tuesday morning, we left by plane for Dalat and came back the next evening. Dalat is one of the cities which the French used as a summer resort. We stayed overnight with the Jacksons and had a good visit. They were wonderful people. We also met Sau and his family who are also mentioned in the book. They are the Montagnard people. Sau took the bracelet off of his arm and put it on mine. This is a sign that we have become friends. He also took a string of beads of his wife's and put it around Mom's neck. He also gave her a second string of beads from his daughter. These people were also spoken of as the tribe's people. The Jacksons have pioneered this work among the tribe's people.

On our way to the airport from Dalat, we saw our planes bombing a VC camp. We saw the bombs leave the plane, and the big puff of smoke when they landed. The communists had blown up a bridge the night before.

So far this month, we have served fifty-nine free home-cooked meals. This is a very important part of our ministry here. You would better understand if you could be here a few days, eat restaurant food, or hear how the men get along out in the battle area.

We are thrilled with the tract work. Recently we met an Air Force doctor with a marvelous testimony. He was saved through a reading of a gospel tract.

Thieves have entered our place twice in the past month while we slept and made away with about $100 worth of food and appliances. They can climb a wall like a mouse. We have put on more locks and asked the landlord to do some more security work.

As I walked down the street a few weeks ago, a man came running toward me, followed by another with a gun in his hand. Within a few feet of me, the second man leveled the gun and fired. The first man got away but my own face and arms were powder burned. So we do get in on a little excitement once in a while.

# November 1967

My straw hat was wearing out. It was the only one I have seen over here. The servicemen said that they know me by my hat. Getting into the small taxis was very hard on a hat.

We are invited to have dinner this evening with Dr. Bob Pierce, who is head of World Vision, Inc. He sponsored a number of orphanages here in the Far East. Perhaps you wondered how we are able to get away from the place the way we do. Well, tonight there are four young men here and they have volunteered to get their own meal. One of the fellows liked to cook. It was good for them to have a place where they can do things like that. It made them feel more like this is their home.

We just received fifteen three-pound cans of cookies from a church in Washington. They were delicious and were packed so nicely that they came through in fine shape.

Mom has gone to the Third Field Hospital to visit this afternoon. She goes there once each week. I am having to stay at the place, as we do not have a helper here, since the one we had got sick and the doctor told her to quit work. We will have a helper here tomorrow. She will stay right here and work for us all the time. She is a real good worker, so we hope that this problem is solved for a while. This will give Mom and me a chance to go to town almost any night to give out tracts. Otherwise, we could only go when we were able to get someone to stay here.

# December 1967

Last week I visited the big hospital in Long Binh, about fifteen miles from Saigon. It has a helicopter pad just across the street. One young man told me that in less than five minutes after the copter picked him up in the field, he was being treated in the hospital.

A serviceman gave me a motorcycle and we went out to the base to see if we could get papers fixed up. I have ridden the motorcycle around the block to see if it is something I can handle before going out on busy streets.

# January 1968

January was a great month in that God saved souls, but in February came the Viet Cong offensive. While the attack was expected, I am sure no one thought it would be in such strength. Last night we were able to see the machine gun fire from the helicopters and fires started in different parts of the city. We saw about everything from the top of our house. We had gone up to the rooftop to record some tapes to send home. The fireworks have started or what we thought was fireworks, but all of a sudden realized, "This is the real thing." It gave one a strange feeling to see machine guns spitting their bullets at the enemy and saw raging fires in various parts of the city. The turn in the war enabled men to be more conscious of their need for God. For several days we were not permitted to leave our house. Now we are allowed to go out between 8:00 a.m. and 7:00 p.m., enabling us to get our mail and to make some contacts.

At this time, there were no servicemen that can come here for any meetings, so we had a lot of time for ourselves. It has given us a chance to catch up on our letter writing and a few things like that. We were really behind because of the Christmas mail and the other things that had to be done about that time.

Maybe you read about the missionaries that were killed at Ban Me Tuot. We knew most of them. We heard that they were going to have a memorial service for them here and then take them back to Ban Me Tuot for burial. This was the second time that the VC has killed missionaries in that place.

They were expecting another attack on Saigon in a few days. All we can do was just wait and see what happens. The Lord has made it possible for us to be in what I consider a very safe area. We were far enough from the Air Base to be safe should it be hit with mortar shells, and we were far enough from the heart of Saigon to escape the attacks that may come there. But we were very cautious and took no chances.

# February 18, 1968

We were both awakened at about 1:00 a.m. We knew just about what was going on, but we couldn't be sure just how strong the attack would be. I went up on the housetop and saw the fires that were started and figured out what the situation was, so I went back to bed and soon fell asleep. I suppose it was a little hard to understand how one could go to sleep when there were explosions going on that shook the house. But to stay awake wouldn't make things any better, so why?

We had a service this morning with three servicemen and two American women were present besides ourselves. We didn't know that anyone would be able to come after what went on last night. But it was so good to have a service and sing the good old gospel songs and hear from God's wonderful Word.

This afternoon, two servicemen came with a jeep and took me to the base to mail a letter and get our mail. It was sure nice to get letters even if we don't do too well in answering.

Our heart had been in this work to such an extent that it was going to be so hard to pull up and leave when we know that the need is so great. We had built up our equipment to the place where we had the things necessary for carrying on the work here. We have been able to gain the respect of the military so that we were accepted by the leadership. This didn't come about overnight. Our pioneer days have been filled with many strange experiences. It took time for us to get our APO privileges and also our commissary and exchange privileges.

# February 21, 1968

Last night, we had three servicemen in for dinner. It seemed good that the men could be coming again. However, this didn't mean that the curfew is lifted for the men on base. The ones that were here were special duty men that were more or less on their own.

I suppose you have heard all about the mortar attacks made on the Tan Son Nhut Air Base. They made a direct hit on the beautiful new chapel that they have recently finished on the Base. The annex where the chaplain's offices are was set on fire. I hadn't gone over to see just how much damage was done. I confined my travels to that which is necessary.

February has slipped by with its horrors and heartaches. We must frankly admit that we did not know what would be the right thing to do at the beginning of the attack. A plane was provided to take the missionaries out. But this work was upon our hearts, and we knew the need to be so great. We felt that we must stay and see how God would work things out. We were glad we stayed. We have had many wonderful opportunities to witness to men in the hospitals.

The night before last, the artillery fire was so heavy that one could hardly sleep. The mortars that the VC sent slamming into the city was anything but soothing to the nerves. Mom and I went to Vung Tau the other day by helicopter and stayed overnight with the Warrens in their service center. They really have a nice place. We came home the next day in one of the army's single-engine nine-passenger planes called the "Otter." It was a very enjoyable trip.

We now feel it was the will of God for us to come to the States for two months. A fine Christian couple took care of the center while we were away, and an Air Force captain did most of the preaching.

# April 1968

We were enjoying a few weeks here in the States. However, the burden of our hearts was for the work in Vietnam. We will be returning on or before May twentieth.

# May 1968

We greet you again from Saigon. We found everything in fine shape at the center. You would rejoice to hear that a Baldwin organ had been given to us. When the Tan Son Nhut Airbase chapel was destroyed by a mortar, the organ was saved. There was only slight damage to the finish.

Rev. Eddie Karnes, director of World Harvesters, Inc., informed us a few days before our return to Saigon that because of other commitments, he would no longer be able to send money for our rent. This meant that we must trust the Lord to raise up others to take up where he had left off. The Lord and His people would not fail. Some people think that money is a problem with God but really it is people who are His problem. One time, Jesus and Peter had a money problem come up. It was a little matter of tribute money. So Jesus said to Peter, "Go to the sea, cast in a hook, and take the fish that first comes up. And when you have opened its mouth, you will find a piece of money" (Matthew 17:27 KJV). Money wasn't the problem. Peter was a net fisherman. He didn't want to fool around with a hook to take one fish at a time, but that was the way Jesus said to do it. What a problem people are to God!

You should have been here yesterday. We had an electrical storm. I don't believe I have ever seen the like. I would really like to know just how much water came down in the hour. I was caught up at the base post office and sure glad to be inside.

Last Thursday, I went by helicopter to Long Binh to visit the big hospital. I took 110 booklets and gave them all out before I had visited all the wards. It was the reward of a lifetime just to get to visit with the men and talk to them about the Lord and have prayer with them. I went down again on Thursday, the Lord willing. There were a lot of men in the hospitals now.

# June 22, 1968

The landlord had agreed to let us pay the rent each month rather than six months in advance. He had asked for our personal check ($400 American money) rather than the sixty-two thousand piasters which would cost $525 at their exchange rate. He banked his money in France, so he must get a very good exchange on it. That was his business. It was much better for us.

I wish I could tell you that there were no more rockets coming into the city of Saigon, but I couldn't. The other night, one hit a house a few blocks from here and killed seven Vietnamese civilians.

President Johnson was pleading for a strong arms control bill. It was certain that no law will keep guns out of the hands of criminals; but when citizens of any country become unarmed, they become preys to their enemies.

One didn't have to live very long in this country to see what could be done to an unarmed citizenry. The Viet Cong could come into any house here and make the people do what they want. The VC came into a home where there was a sixteen- or seventeen-year-old boy and asked the parents to let him fight on the Viet Cong side. If they refuse, one of the small children of the home will be shot before the parents' eyes. If they still protest, another will be shot. It didn't take much of that to get the parents' consent. Many people accused the South Vietnamese of being disloyal to their government. But people could be made to do things they didn't want to do when they have a gun at their backs.

# June 18, 1968

*From Mom Kincaid*

We just had our daily downpour, so now we opened the shutters. Dad would soon leave for the base. He went to Long Binh early yesterday on the helicopter to visit our servicemen in the hospital. To us, it was still a miracle that we could be here to do this work.

Some support had been discontinued but we feel confident the rent money would always be here when due. You see, dear children, we talked of faith in God, taking Him at his Word. Now, we had another opportunity to prove Him.

And if this practically new Baldwin organ wasn't a miracle! You couldn't buy an organ here if you had a fortune!

# July 3, 1968

The young man who preached the Sunday morning service poured out his heart concerning the need of professing Christians. Many came over here not knowing the first thing about salvation. They knew they were supposed to pray, but to them, it was only saying words that they trust would do some good. They were surprised that it was possible to have a personal relationship with God.

Lord willing, I would be going to Long Binh tomorrow to visit the Twenty-Fourth Evacuation Hospital. Next week, I would go to the other one, which was the Ninety-Third Evacuation Hospital.

I must get out to the helicopter port as early as possible to get my name on the list. They were all stand-by flights. When a ship came in that was going where you wanted to go, they start at the top of the list and called a name for every seat available. The nearer one's name was to the top of the list, the quicker he could go. Sometimes I had to wait for two hours for a ten to twelve-minute ride.

Since Tet, the army buses, did not run on very good schedules. They did not go onto the base as they did before, because the drivers were Vietnamese.

# July 4, 1968

Our Independence Day at home. Today I heard what sounded like an explosion close by. Then I heard a truck in front of our place. I decided that I better go out and see what it was all about. It happened to be two servicemen bringing us about fifteen cases of pop! It was sure nice to have some in the refrigerator when the fellows dropped in on a hot afternoon.

# July 11, 1968

*I* was at Long Binh today. There were a lot of hepatitis cases in the hospital. After one saw what some of the fellows were going through, he was thankful to be alive and had good health.

While I was gone today, Mom baked a cherry and an apple pie. They were really good!

We had company to share our supper, a major in the Air Force who had been recently converted. He was so hungry for the things of God. I was amazed at his progress. He was trying to drink in all that he could before he went back to the States (about fifty days yet).

# July 16, 1968

*I* went to a Chinese optometrist to get new glasses. I tried to make him understand that I wanted trifocals. He had made two pairs, and I hadn't been able to wear either one. My old glasses were really very good yet. At least they seemed better since I had tried the others.

# July 30, 1968

*To Our Dear Family*

There is a serviceman in California who will be sending you three boxes for us. He took them to the States in his "hole" baggage. They were allowed four hundred pounds baggage from here when they went home, and he didn't have that much, so he took these things for us. There was a tea set, a wooden salad bowl set, and a carved water buffalo.

It had been a busy day. We started early to get our new ID cards which we were to have by August 1, but we ended up at the wrong place. Mom did Red Cross work today, so there was no time to go to the right place.

August 1 was our fortieth anniversary as you had remembered, dear ones. August 23 would be my sixty-eighth birthday. I received a card which read, "Don't worry about growing old. Many are denied the privilege." But Mom and I did not have time to worry about growing old; we were so busy helping these young men stay alive.

We had survived the enemy's hardest efforts to take Saigon. Our military had placed a strong security force around the perimeter of the city in an effort to prevent rocket attacks. We hope it worked.

We must frankly admit that we had gone through some dangerous times these past months. But at no time did we feel like running from our responsibility. We were now able to minister in three hospitals and reached more than one hundred new men each week.

# August 29, 1968

*From Mom to the Family*

I went to the hospital yesterday to see Lan's wife and baby (Vietnamese). I didn't find them, but I did see about one hundred very small babies in incubators. The incubators were given to this country by the United States.

# August 30, 1968

*To the Dear Family*

We were all enthused about daughter Nancy and family coming, so it was a bit disappointing when they couldn't. But we did know that this was no place for a family to live at present. It was all for the best that it turned out as it had. I was sure Nancy was disappointed too after suffering through all the shots and making her plans. She could had been a lot of help to us.

Mom and I did get a little lonesome at times. But being busy so much of the time we couldn't dwell on being lonesome.

There had been a tenseness in Saigon lately because they had expected some kind of an attack. I hoped the Viet Cong were never able to send any more rockets into the city.

This morning, a young serviceman took Mom to the commissary in an open jeep, and it started to rain. She got as wet as though she had fallen into the river, but it was so warm it didn't bother one much.

Now Mom was getting set for a game of Scrabble with a young fellow, so I'd keep to my writing except to stop and to fry a couple of wieners for his sandwich.

# August 1968

Recently a Red Cross worker came to Mom lamenting the fact that her life seemed empty and meaningless. Mom was able to lead her to Christ. Now she was a changed person with the joy of the Lord on her countenance.

Many of the men had asked us who our sponsor was. They could hardly believe that we had no individual or group wholly responsible for our support and that we were just supported by those back home who cared. People back in the States did realize, regardless of whether the war was justifiable in their minds or not, that our men were here and needed our help.

We received many anniversary cards, and we thank you. I spent the day visiting men in the Ninety-Third Evacuation Hospital, while Mom took care of things here at the center.

Do pray for a speedy end to this war, for the men who must be away from their families, and for us that we may always do God's will.

# September 2, 1968

*Pop to the Family*

Everyone had been expecting another big Viet Cong attack. Waiting for it to happen was as bad as living through one in some ways. There was sniping on the streets of Saigon. So far it had not been servicemen who had been killed, but it made one realize that just to be an American could be dangerous. We stayed off the streets as much as we could, but one couldn't crawl into a hole and stay there.

Did we tell you that one could not get into the PX or commissary without an ID card? According to the military directive, it was impossible for us to get any, but thanks be to God, both of us had our ID cards!

Big tall Rodrick Gabbert had returned to the States. The man who led him to Christ, Drew Boucke, would leave the last of the month. They would be traveling through Oregon and Washington. If they happen to come by your place, take good care of them. They had been so good to us. Drew would be married soon after he gets home. Then he would go to Washington, DC, where he would be working in the Pentagon.

# September 15, 1968

*Mom to the Family*

A beautiful day…as long as the big fan kept going. I didn't think I had the sheet over me all last night.

We've just had breakfast. Dad had corn flakes and applesauce, and I had Pop-Tarts and applesauce. You see, our captain was in port again. He had the large marine ship that brought frozen food, and he gave us our first fresh apples since we had been in Vietnam.

We were so happy yesterday to get my mother's letter and to hear of all that was done for her on her ninetieth birthday. Thank you all for the part you had in it.

What a day yesterday! Almost a full house for morning service. When Drew gave the invitation, Doug and Peter went upfront. You see, these young men had been weighing this for months. Then Dad baptized Drew, Doug, Peter, John, Eddie, and the Red Cross worker. This was one of the things that made it possible for us to toil on in this land of uncertainties. Later the newly baptized came back for dinner, fourteen in all. A blessed day.

John was saved a week ago (Saturday), and he was already praying with and for others, trying to help them know Christ.

# September 30, 1968

*Pop to the Family*

It was nothing but a miracle the way the Lord had undertaken for things that looked insurmountable. We operated on $800 per month.

Meat was so very expensive at the commissary. We had our freezer back, and we were just waiting for someone to kill a water buffalo.

Mom was giving out tracts in the commissary the other day. A young man said to her, "Lady, would you like to have me help you give out those tracts? I'm a Catholic, and that tract would make anyone want to go to church." People over here soon realized that it was the Lord and not a denomination that was needed.

Ever since we had been in this place, Mom had wanted some lawn chairs to use on our roof in the evenings. Last week, the commissary had what she wanted. So I bought her one for her birthday and she bought me one for mine. About 9:30 last night, after everyone had left, we took our chairs to the roof. As we relaxed there and mused at the privilege of having this great ministry, it almost overwhelmed us.

The box of envelopes that we asked to be sent to us had arrived. So now we must cut five hundred pieces of waxed paper to put under the flap of each one or they would all be stuck together as the humidity was so great here.

Mom visited one of the day schools that was run by the Church of Christ people. She was told that they needed teachers, so she said that she would be willing to come sometimes as a substitute teacher. They took her at her word and came after her to teach while one of the teachers was in the hospital. She enjoyed the work, but it really put us behind with our work so much that she just had to quit. But she did have one period in which she could tell the children a Bible story. She sure enjoyed doing that.

# November 21, 1968

Mom was over at the International School teaching English this evening, so I would try to write a bit. I left early this morning to visit the Ninety-Third Evacuation Hospital at Long Binh. I really had a good day. Got a ride down there in a little four-man helicopter. It was a really great way of getting around. When I got off at headquarters, they furnished me a taxi to go the three miles, more or less, to the hospital. Then I was on my feet a lot as I went from bed to bed. I gave out just about one hundred of the little booklets, "Here's How" today, so you could see about how many men I got to visit with. Last Tuesday, I expanded our ministry to reach as many men for the Lord as we possibly could.

> **As we reached out and were blessed to see a serviceman accept Christ as Lord and Savior, I thought of my own experience of conversion to Christ so many years ago. In August of 1923, a prayer group in Powers, Oregon, invited Rev. Harry R. Neat to hold revival services in a tent on a vacant lot on the main street of Powers, Oregon.**
>
> **Some young people invited me to the meetings, which I accepted just a few days before the meetings closed. The very first service convinced me that I should be a Christian, but how could that be?**

Walking back to the logging camp that night by myself, I did some very serious thinking. I had to walk five miles up the railroad track to the camp, where I stayed.

As I walked along on this beautiful moonlit night, I thought of my cigarette habit. I knew Christ would never allow himself to be in bondage to such a habit, but how was I to be free from it? I had tried to quit several times but failed each time. But the thought of prayer came to my mind, however, I knew nothing about praying. All I could think to do was to look up to heaven and ask God to take the gnawing appetite for tobacco away from me. So I just looked up and said, "God, if you want me to be a Christian, you will have to take this gnawing appetite for tobacco away from me." When I had said that it seemed that I was overshadowed by such a sweet and restful presence. It seemed that my body was floating. My whole being was so restful. I was afraid to even think lest I would spoil this wonderful experience which did finally lift from me. But my desire for tobacco was forever gone from me.

The next day was a wonderful day to me. I felt a freedom that was wonderful, but I was so anxious to get back to the meeting, for I knew there was something more for me. I must give my heart and life to the Lord. As I sat in the meeting that night, I could hardly wait for the preacher to get through and give the invitation for those wanting to accept Christ to come forward. When the invitation did come, I didn't wait to see if anyone else was going or not but stepped out for God. As I knelt at the altar, I didn't know how to pray, but I knew what I wanted. I wanted a new life, and that was just what I got. As those that prayed with me told me that God would forgive all my sins and give me a new life, the joy and glory of God filled my soul. When I got up from the altar, everything was different. Everything looked different. There came a joy into my life that has never departed but ever springs up in my soul.

The special meetings closed the following Sunday with a water baptismal service in the afternoon in the nearby river. As I remembered, there were fifty of us that were baptized that afternoon. This was a wonderful experience for me. It seemed that it was revealed to me how I should walk a new life from that day forward.

Well, we didn't have our telephone hooked up yet, but it looked like it was going to be before long now. A man told me that he thought he would have a generator for us before long. So we would just "wait and see," that was the way we live over here. Our electricity had been doing quite well lately, but it would be good to have a generator here just in case it did fail.

This had been a big day, so I guess this had better come to a close. We received a package of cookies and things from Nancy the other day. The cookies were a bit shaken up, but they are just the kind I like, so they would be eaten.

# January 1969

Last Monday I took quite a trip. I was supposed to go to Bien Hoa to locate a young man that had just come over here. His father had written to the Assemblies of God Servicemen's Division to see if they had a Chaplain in the area. Since they didn't, they wrote to me about it. I was unable to get a flight direct to Bien Hoa. At twelve thirty, I was able to go by plane, but the plane had to go down into the Delta first to pick up a couple of colonels and to take them to Bien Hoa. So I was privileged to see a lot of the country that I had never seen before. I didn't have my camera, but I would sure take it the next time. I did find the young man and had a good visit with him. I came home by helicopter. It had to go up North to Phlu Loi before coming to Saigon, so I was able to see some of the level and fertile land here.

# February 1969

We would like to introduce you to Lt. Col. Clair A. McCombs, who wrote the following testimony just before leaving for the States.

I thank God for bringing me to Vietnam. Not because I wanted to come because I did not. I have five fine children and a wonderful wife in the States and I enjoy every minute I can spend with them. However, I've learned that so often it isn't the times of enjoyment that we mature in our Christian experiences, but it's often the times of testing—the difficult times—the times alone where our Lord can teach us things that He cannot when we are at our ease. I think of Psalm 84:5–6, "Blessed is the man whose strength is in Thee: in whose heart are the ways of them. Who passing through the valley of Baca make it a well; the rain also filleth the pools." And what a well or spring is the servicemen's center here in this dry place, this desert of hearing the Word of God preached. Yes, Mom and Pop Kincaid have raised up, for the glory of God, a refreshing place where Christ is above everything else, a place where the Holy Spirit can speak to hearts, a place where a dedicated man and woman of God dwell, with whom one can share spiritual needs and life's problems. It's also a place like home, where good music can be heard, where you can sit down to a home-cooked meal. A place where I thank God for and which I thank all of you for making possible for men such as I because of such as Jesus who loved us so.

Sincerely in His care,<br>(Signed) Lt. Col. Clair A. McCombs USAF

Just last week, I met a young man that had been shot through the thigh, shattering the bone and severing the blood vessels. I asked him if he was a Christian, and he said, "I sure am.

When I was hit, I began to pray. They kept shooting at me trying to finish me off but not another bullet would hit me." At first, the doctors didn't think they could save his leg. But a man with such faith couldn't lose. I was glad I could pray with him and encourage him.

We haven't had an apple pie for the men lately as Mom's electric oven had burned out. Our electric current was so irregular that it was very hard on appliances. We priced the butane stoves with ovens and found that they cost $150.00 to $200.00. A young evangelist, who was visiting here at the time, promised us that he would raise the money for us when he returned to the States in about one month. Please pray that he would be able to keep his promise.

As you must know from the news, there were mortar shells coming into Saigon now. Please pray for our safety. The men needed us more now than ever. So, we must be at our post of duty.

# May 1969

At last, we had a telephone. It was wonderful to have a phone if necessary.

The young man that installed the phone accepted Christ before he left the center. The next day, he told us that as he laid on his bed that night, he thought about what a good thing it was to be a Christian.

There were many fine young men in the hospitals here now. I wish it were possible for you to make one trip with me to a hospital. I was to the men a civilian chaplain. It touched my heart to have them cling to my hand and hardly let me go after praying with them.

# June 1969

A new hospital had been opened to our ministry. This was a new one built on the Tan Son Nhut Air Base, where men were treated just before they were to be sent to Japan or the States or some other place out of Vietnam. I think Mom would be going there about twice each week. I visited the hospital at Lai Khe last week for the first time and would love to go there often, but transportation was not always available to me. We sincerely believed that our hospital work alone was worth all that it cost to keep us over here.

This word of testimony from one of the young men that had returned to the States might be of interest to you. "Pop, the Bible that you gave me is my best friend, and I am learning a lot from it, although I sure wish that I could sit with you and Mom and have you explain to me that which I don't understand. But you have taught me that I have an even better friend, and the best teacher of all, Jesus."

Mom went with me to Cu Chi, last week, to visit the two hospitals there. Cu Chi was near the Cambodian border and not many civilians ventured up there. It was not such an easy trip. We left here before 7:00 a.m. We must take a taxi up to one hundred yards of the Air Base gate. That was as far as the taxi was allowed to go. We walked through the gate then thumbed a ride to the helicopter port. Once we were on board, the flight to Cu Chi by helicopter took about twenty minutes. From the heliport in Cu Chi to the first hospital was about one mile. We were able to get a man to take us there in a jeep. After we had visited all the men in the wards, they took us by ambulance to the other hospital which was about a half or three-quarters of a mile away. This was a much larger hospital. We visited the wards there until noon. After lunch, we visited the two extensive care wards and were able to get through just in time to catch a ride to Saigon in a helicopter that was taking a seriously wounded man to the Third Field Hospital here. I made this trip once each week. I saw and heard of many needs for a God-honoring ministry here. For instance, while trying to encourage a young man that had lost both legs, he looked up at me and said, "Can God give me a new mind?" This revealed how great the mental strain is, and what confusion this war had brought to our young men. I was glad I could tell him, "Yes, God can give you a new mind." God had told us that to be carnally minded is death, but to be spiritually minded is life and peace. See Romans 8:6, 1 Corinthians 2:16, and Philippians 2:5.

We have had several very important missionary visitors this past month, Rev. Aaron Rothganger, Rev. Lester Sumrall, Evangelist Hal Herman and his wife, and Evangelist Billy Graham. It was always such a blessing and uplift to us to have someone come along to minister.

A company, which had a large office building near us, had run a line from their big generator to our place. So now we would never be without electricity when the Vietnamese power went off which was very often. This was unsolicited help. The manager had been observing our work here and wanted to help. God was so good to us. I was sure that very few of us had ever experienced all the good things God would like to do for us if we would fully trust Him.

Roderick had been able to help us a lot here in the center. There was always plenty to do. Through a Vietnamese army captain, he knew during his year in the service here, he had been able to witness each week to the boys and some older men in the correction house. These were mostly orphaned, juvenile delinquents. Through his witnessing, several had professed Christ. The problem of a good follow-up system was something we wanted you to pray about.

## August 1969

Mom was out to the Cholon BX to give out eighty of the little booklets "Here's How" and perhaps buy a few things there. We could buy in the BX and PX what few things they had, but we still couldn't buy in the commissary. But there was always a way to get along.

We have had another anniversary, forty-first. I took Mom out to dinner at the Caraville Hotel.

## September 1969

We must tell you that we were both well and very happy that we were able to be a help to the fine American men that were over here in, what so many call, a senseless war. We never could be able to tell you in words the full extent of our ministry over here. I could never fully tell you how I felt when I stood by the side of a wounded young man in a hospital bed. God had enabled me to look at him as my own son and my heart went out to him in love and compassion. It was so easy to pray for them and talk with them about the things of God.

I was sitting in the A & D Office of the Twelfth Evacuation Hospital at Cu Chi. I had been able to lead three young men to accept Christ and had been able to pray with many others. I was now waiting for a ride back to Saigon.

We had seen a miracle this last month. One rainy day, when returning from the post office with our mail in my briefcase, I forgot to take my briefcase out of the taxi. When I discovered this, I was horrified. Mom spoke up and said, "All we can do is pray." In about two hours, a taxi drove up with my briefcase and all the contents. In this country, this just had to be a miracle. Praise God for miracles.

Roderick had left for the States where he would enter Bible College. We would miss him so very much.

I had a testimony from a young man concerning his experience in Vietnam which I thought you would enjoy reading.

I had graduated from college and taken a
job teaching at High Mowing School. There

would be no need to go to Vietnam. I could be deferred until my age would no longer qualify me for service. Yet, feeling somehow, I should go into the service, I explored the branches. Taking a test for Air Force, they accepted me as an officer candidate and then found I would have to wait a year for admission. My need was immediate, and I found the idea of waiting intolerable. Further, it had begun to be important, again for no clearly explainable reason, to go into the service as an enlisted man. Only a few days after hearing from the Air Force, I enlisted for the draft, throwing myself, as it were, to fortune's fancy. Then things moved rapidly, basic training, Army Intelligence School, and finally Vietnam. A diary I kept for a few months at the start of my Vietnam tour records that by Sunday, November 5th, I had met Drew Boucke and talked with him about religion to about midnight that night. Thus began my first confrontation with religion. By the end of November, I had been to the Saigon Christian Servicemen's Center, the first of many wonderful times there. The days kept dropping from my short timer's calendar and slowly, almost imperceptibly, I was growing. Mom and Pop, wise with patience, watched, occasionally softly speaking with love of their feeling for Christ. Then close to a year ago this day, on September 15, 1968, the same Drew Boucke I had met early in my tour gave the Sunday service. At its end, he asked if there was anyone who wanted to testify his belief in Christ…and there I was, standing beside this person with a smile that would have held a watermelon. I publicly gave my life to Christ that day. Odd as it may seem, Drew did also, for we both had come to Christ, me for the first time, and Drew in a more meaningful way than ever before.

There were others that day too, Pete, Charlotte, and more yet who I had not known but are now somehow specially related as we were all reborn that day.

I look now to the fifteenth of September as a more meaningful birthday than that one which first dropped me into the world's population figures. My prayers will remember you as I celebrate this day of being born again and I hope you will remember it with happiness too."

Faithfully yours, Signed Doug

# October 2, 1969

Mom went up to Nha Trang yesterday to visit the Morgans who ran a servicemen's center there. I had been there, but this was Mom's first time. We would have loved to go together, but someone had to stay here and take care of the place. Mom really needed a little time away from the steady grind here. She should be back here in a few minutes now. I was sorry that we didn't have a car so that I could meet her when the plane came in. But she would thumb her way home. The servicemen were very good to be a help to us.

Perhaps you would enjoy reading the following testimony of Major Ernest Varney.

> I began my tour at Phuoc Vin, Vietnam, in an Assault Helicopter Company. For the first time in my Christian experience of three years, I was without Christian fellowship. Prayer that God would send another Christian to my unit was answered by my being transferred to Saigon after only six weeks in country. A short time after being in Saigon, Al Sligh invited me to a Saturday night service at the Christian Servicemen's Center. What a spiritual blessing that service was to my heart! What fellowship! What joy divine! Praise the Lord! Brothers bubbling over with love for the Savior and for each other. Worship in freedom with only God's blessing being sought.

I could not get over these two servants of the Master coming to such a place and their serenity and dedication amazed me each time I walked the alley leading to the house they had set up for God's use. The house was not located where the present center is, and one has to actually go there to appreciate the remoteness and the danger. We returned again and again, drawn together by a single bond of faith and love in the Lord Jesus. We came singing praises to God and left the same way. We witnessed by word, tract, and example. We visited the sick and wounded, we cried for the lost, we lived for those precious hours when we could be together again at the center for physical and spiritual rest. It was a mountain top experience. But we are not permitted to remain on the mountains. There came another valley to go through. I was transferred to Chu Lai, far to the north, and there I spent the last five months of my tour. I kept in touch with the brethren at the center and was sustained by their faithful prayers. My last visit to the center came as I was departing Vietnam. I spent three lovely days with the Kincaids sharing the new Christian home they had established. What a wonderful reunion we had. There were beautiful scenes such as the night Sam Marshall came to the center and upon seeing me, ran to me, threw his arms around me, and with tears streaming down his face, exclaimed, "Oh! Brother Ernest, how we have prayed for you." I have written about only a tiny portion of the blessings and experiences I shared at the Christian Servicemen's Center. I believe in the work being done by Mom and Pop. They are living their lives for Jesus. They are doing what our heavenly Father has commanded them to do. Those who contribute to this work are doing what He has commanded them to do. May God bless you as you share in this vital ministry. "The Lord watch between me and thee, when we are absent one from another" (Genesis 31:49).

During one of my hospital visitations, the son of an Episcopalian minister told me he had believed the Bible until he went to college and studied philosophy, psychology, and science. I told him that true science proves the Bible.

"Do you know the Bible indicated the world was round long before the time of Columbus?" I quoted Isaiah 40:22 (KJV). He didn't know that was in the Bible.

"How does the weatherman guess what the weather will be?" I asked.

"By barometric pressure," he said.

"Agreed. Do you know the Bible said that more than one thousand years before Christ was born?" I quoted Job 28:25–26 (KJV).

"Do you know when it was that scientists discovered that the moon does not give off light of itself? Job knew that also." I quoted Job 25:5 (KJV).

I suggested he write his parents that he was accepting Christ as his own personal Savior. "Will you do it?"

"Yes, I will," he said, as tears welled up in his eyes.

# November 1969

There was an Assembly of God pastor from Beaumont, Texas, coming over here to hold a revival for the Vietnamese people the second week in December. I had just made arrangements for him to use one of the big French churches for the meetings. He and his wife had been here with us, and at that time he was impressed with the need of reaching the Vietnamese people with the Pentecostal message. We felt that it was God's time for a real breakthrough here. Many of the Vietnamese were getting hungry for more of God.

Well, Thanksgiving had passed. It was really a wonderful day for us here even if I did have to stay in bed most of the day. I came down with a terrible cold and wasn't able to be of any help to Mom, but you know how capable she is at putting other people to work. Well, she got along just fine and had a wonderful dinner prepared by 6:30 p.m. I came down and joined the fourteen others at mealtime. I was in bed just about all day yesterday but was much better. Was able to take a hot shower last night before going to bed. I hadn't shaved all this time, so I told Mom this morning that I had such a good start for a mustache that I thought I would let it grow—but I didn't.

# January 1970

On a recent trip to one of the hospitals, I met a young man in the extensive care ward that had never known Christ as his personal Savior. As I talked with him, I felt impressed by the Lord to ask him if he would like to become a Christian. He said, "Yes I would, if I only knew how." I then told him how to receive Christ and asked him if we could pray together. He was ready to pray and ask Christ to come into his heart and life. As I moved on down the ward, I found a man that had lost a leg. He had such a radiant smile that I said to him, "You must be a Christian."

He said, "Yes, I am." Then he told me how God had spoken to him about the ministry, but he had always turned his head. But when he was hit on the battlefield, he turned and listened to God and had said, "Yes." While he had lost a leg, he had found the peace and joy of the Lord. He was not grieving over his loss, for he had found something of unspeakable value.

# February 1970

We were entering the week of Tet, or the lunar New Year as was celebrated by the Vietnamese on February sixth. It was at this time in 1968 that the VCs made the vicious attack on Saigon. There were some people feeling that there would be some trouble this year. We could only trust the Lord for His protection.

We were privileged to attend the dedication of a new Vietnamese army chapel. The greater part of the money for this building was sent from the States. There were many very fine Christian men in the Vietnamese army.

We would like to tell you about a young man that came to us the last week in February. He had been out in a real firefight where it looked like there was no chance for survival. The radioman froze at the controls and was unable to call for help. This young man had to knock him out so that he could radio for help, thus, they were saved. But this young man was so shaken by this experience that he was sent to Saigon for a few days of rest.

He was a very bewildered young man when he came to us. He said he had once known Christ as his Savior but had gone back into sin. He had been told that once he had been saved, he never could be lost. But he said that he knew that no one living in sin, as he was, could be fit for heaven. We were able to take him to the Bible and show him how God could and would save him from his sins and give him the power to live victoriously each day. He left the center with the peace and joy of the Lord showing upon his face. This was what we live for over here.

We received many letters from the States in which were requests for us to visit a son or a husband who might need encouragement. A wife wrote that she hadn't heard from her husband for a long time and wanted us to check to see what the trouble might be. We found that this man worked on a ship at the Saigon port. As I was walking along the dock on this hot afternoon, a young Vietnamese slipped up behind me and snatched my watch off of my arm. I immediately took after him. Just as I was getting up close, he put the watch in his mouth and jumped into the muddy water. I saw him go down out of sight but never did see him come up any place although I waited five or more minutes.

# April 1970

*R*ev. and Mrs. B. H. Clendennen of Beaumont, Texas, were with us for nearly three weeks. He ministered to us here at the center many times and brought great refreshing to our hearts. God had laid a great burden upon his heart for the Vietnamese people. He was able to preach in many of their churches. The Vietnamese people were becoming very greatly concerned about the need of a revival in this land.

While the Clendennens were here to look after the center, we took two days off and went up to Nah Trang for a little badly needed rest.

Some evenings when the day was done, everyone in bed or gone home, we went up on to the roof, sat on our easy chairs and say, "Oh, we just wish all our children could see us over here, and how the Lord blesses and cares for us."

Mom just said to be sure and thank all of you for all you have done to make it possible for us to keep this home open for our servicemen. Every day or so, we hear them saying things like, "This is certainly an oasis in a desert," or "Thank God for this lighthouse." So we thank all of you who are helping us keep the doors of this home open.

# May/June 1970

God had helped us to keep our health and keep up with our work. But we certainly did realize the need for a rest. And it looked like that was going to be possible.

Many of you would remember Roderick that came over to help us. He and his wife had said that they would come over and take care of the place during the summer vacation so that we may come home for a visit and rest. He had been here with us and knew just how important this place was to the servicemen. They were willing to trust God for their fare over and support while here. I know you would pray for this young couple and for us that we may be able to come home.

Perhaps the following testimony will help you to better understand why this home was needed.

> I'm a Christian, twenty-one years of age, serving a two-year agreement with the United States Army, presently on a twelve-month tour in Vietnam.
>
> Upon arriving in Vietnam, I was rather depressed with a feeling of self-pity. I soon discovered an oasis in a desert—the Christian Servicemen's Center—run by two Christ-filled people, Ma and Pa Kincaid. My sorrowful emotions were changed into joyful ones, thank God.
>
> I believe that the Kincaid's major purpose for being in this land is to meet the spiritual

needs of our fellow brothers and sisters by bringing them to know and accept Christ as their very own personal savior. Yes, they are accomplishing this, their major goal each day whether it be in a hospital visiting the sick or in a postal exchange distributing religious pamphlets, allowing no opportunity of winning souls for Christ to slip by.

To me the servicemen's center is happiness in good home cooked meals, association with other Christian friends, new faces, a place of worship to our Lord, an escape from the noisy city life to an atmosphere of love, peace and tranquility, sharing testimonies with others, Bible studying, praying together for loved ones, singing hymns or praises to God, the luxury of silence to meditate or read, play a game of Scrabble, knowing there's a good listening and wise spiritual counselor to aid oneself, and a chance to grow in Christ!

Before accepting Jesus, I disliked attending church, finding the services boring until I drifted from God completely. Now I hate to leave the services at the center since they bring me so much closer to God. I know I'm not alone in my feelings—praise the Lord!

(Signed) Bill

## September 1970

We are very sorry that we were not able to visit all the churches that extended us an invitation. After we were in the States for a week or so, I had a sick spell that laid me up for a little over a week. We realized then that if the trip home was to do for us what it was intended, we must slow up. We hope everyone would understand and not feel we passed them by intentionally.

While in Los Angeles, California, visiting Mom's ninety-two-year-old mother, a friend took me to a Thrifty Drug Store that was on Whittier Blvd in East Los Angeles. Just as we got to the intersection, we saw fellows taking jewelry out of a broken showcase. We drove around behind the drug store and parked the car. By the time we got back to the front of the store, things were really going bad. Young fellows were standing out in the street throwing bottles through the plate glass windows of stores across the street. On the corner where we were standing, there was a newspaper vending machine, they tipped that over and stomped it to pieces. Someone yelled, "White man, you had better get inside." We could see that there was a real spirit of hate building up. One could sense the very spirit of anti-Christ and rebellion in such a thing. By this time, they had the drug store locked up, so we went back to the car and drove up to another shopping area. We saw police cars with their windows broken out, so it was very evident the police didn't have much control.

It was time for us to head back to Saigon, Vietnam. We would be flying on the 747 as far as Tokyo with a stay over one night in Hawaii.

We were home in Saigon. We were sure this was where the Lord would have us to be.

We landed in Saigon Friday evening, September fourth, and found a good number of servicemen here to welcome us home. We were somewhat weary from the long plane ride, but we found everything going well at the center. We had a good meeting Saturday evening. A number of men had gathered to pray with and bid farewell to a young man who had finished his tour of duty here and was going home. Reverend Richards of Hong Kong was with us for this time of fellowship. His ministry was such a great blessing to all.

We had a wonderful service at the center Sunday morning. It was the last service that Roderick and his wife could be with us as their plane left that afternoon.

# October 1970

It was so wonderful to know that in Jesus, we had the victory always. We were glad to be able to report that the Lord was blessing here at the center in Saigon. We were so thankful to be back, and to do all we could to help these young men know Christ and the joy and peace He could give to all who would receive Him.

The following testimony would help you understand what we meant.

> I remember very clearly my anxiety as my twenty-six-hour flight to Vietnam was nearing an end. The land below was a colorful patchwork of green and brown yet my thoughts were pointed towards the future and what the Lord had in store for the year to come.
>
> My heart had been given to Jesus three years before, and He has been "the master of my ship, the captain of my fate" since then. When my orders for duty in Vietnam arrived, I knew that it was His will, and my life was absolutely safe in His hands. My earnest prayer was for a strong body of believers with which I could grow and work for the Lord. Within a week after I had arrived, the Lord led me to the Saigon Christian Servicemen's Center. The fellowship of dedicated Christian servicemen and the personal ministries

of Mom and Pop Kincaid have been a tremendous answer to prayer.

So many things are happening here that it would be too time consuming to record them all. But briefly, a Korean soldier, an American sailor, a young Chinese woman, and the Vietnamese maid here at the Center, have all recently found a new faith in Jesus. I thank and praise the Lord for this opportunity to serve and be a witness to the work He is performing here in Vietnam. (LT. JG. James Sutherland)

Once again, we were taking the helicopters to get out to the hospitals to visit the men there. It was interesting to fly over the rice paddies and rubber plantations. The men were so receptive to the gospel message. They seemed to appreciate a civilian coming in and showing interest in them. We were also glad to report that there are less American servicemen in the hospitals now.

We had been able to give out many thousands of the little booklet "Here's How," which had been furnished to us by Life Messengers of Seattle, Washington.

We were having more men coming to the center now than we have ever had. So it was very evident that we were needed here for some time yet.

During our time in Vietnam, we had met many wonderful Vietnamese people. Some very noble people became close friends. There were many that had come as refugees from North Vietnam because they didn't want to live under communism. They were willing to sacrifice all they had and were starting life anew in South Vietnam where they hoped to be free to exercise their ability to progress in a land that they hoped would always be free. However, there were many in South Vietnam that would care less what kind of a government they were living under just so they could have a bowl of rice. This would be one of the problems of ever establishing a strong democratic government in South Vietnam.

When we first started the field hospital visitations, we had to go by helicopter and had to be on a standby basis. But later when it was known what our ministry meant to the servicemen, we were able to go on scheduled flights. This saved us time and enabled us to visit more men. I was respected as a civilian chaplain and was given many privileges as an officer.

Every man I visited in the hospital was given one of the little tracts/booklets entitled, "Here's How." And if he needed a Bible or New Testament, we did our best to supply him with one. I could only carry a limited number with me each day.

All our work was nondenominational. We never let anyone's church affiliation keep us from trying to encourage them in their faith toward God. I remembered going into the extensive care unit of one of the hospitals one day. As was my custom, I inquired of the nurse in charge if there was anyone there that I could visit with. She said, "Yes, I wish you would talk to this young man," as she pointed to a bed.

I said to her, "It looks like he is asleep."

She said, "If he is, we will wake him up." He was a fine-looking young man. I would judge him to be about twenty-five years of age. I could see he had lost both legs close up to his body.

I spoke to him and introduced myself to him as a minister. He looked up at me and said, "I am a Catholic." Which could have meant he felt our church relationship could be a barrier between us.

I quickly said to him, "Your faith in God is your greatest asset, hold on to that." I sensed that this caused him to relax a bit. Then I said to him, "God loves you," and I then quoted John 3:16. I told him that God had spared his life because He had something good in life for him. I told him that if he would keep his life dedicated to God, he could yet have a wonderful life in spite of any handicap he might feel he had. I quoted to him many scriptures concerning God's care for those that would freely trust in Him through their faith in Jesus Christ as Savior. I could see that he was trying to grasp every word. I felt that if the religious barriers were broken down, and he could see that I was only trying to strengthen his faith in the Lord, and if I were to offer to pray for him, he would accept my offer. When I asked him if he would like me to pray for him, he said an enthusiastic yes. My heart went out in real earnest prayer for that young man.

Mom had a wonderful tract ministry. She made a trip once each week to the commissary where she would give out the little booklet, "Here's How." She would take over one hundred of these each trip. She never had to carry any of them back home.

During a time when the commissary was closed to seventy-five percent of the servicemen because of black market activities, she was able to give out these booklets in the PX at Cholon. One day the gatekeeper informed her that she could no longer give out her booklets. She asked who had given such orders and was told that the manager had given the order. She then asked to see the manager. She found him to be an American Japanese, who was a Buddhist. He went to great lengths to explain to her why she could not be permitted to give out her booklet. She asked him who it was that gave him such orders. He gave her the name of the colonel, so she decided to go see him. His receptionist questioned her as to why she wanted to see him and told her that she would let Mom know if an appointment could be made. Mom left one of the booklets for the colonel to examine.

The next day, she received a telephone call from a man that was supposed to be speaking for the colonel explaining why permission could not be granted for her to give out her booklets in the PX or commissary. She thought this was final but prayed for God to have His way. She only waited a few minutes until the phone rang. When she answered, it was the colonel himself speaking. He asked her if she could come to his office at 10:00 a.m. the next day, and of course, she told him she could. The next day she was there at the appointed time and was received graciously by the colonel. He inquired about the work of the center and about all our activities in Vietnam. She wondered what the outcome of all this would be especially after the other telephone call. She could only breathe a prayer. Soon the colonel gave his testimony of faith in God and how he had been a Christian for many years. He also told her that he had read the booklet she had left in his office. He said the little booklet, "Here's How" was good enough for anyone to read. He then told her that he was sending word to those in charge of the PX that she should be allowed to give out her booklets in the PX at any time. So the problem was solved. Another miracle of God on behalf of the work!

In carrying on a work like this in a foreign land presents many problems. When the black-market situation reached a point where the military had to close the commissary to more than seventy-five percent of the servicemen, we were also cut off. We were still permitted to buy in the PX, but a very limited amount of food was available there. Only God could open up for us ways whereby we could keep up our supply. It was a miracle to us the way God supplied. We would be able to get what was needed by some branch of the armed services that found themselves overstocked with just what we needed, and they would bring it in to us. We became acquainted with the manager of the USO. He would sell us some hard-to-get things which would tide us over until a new supply would come in.

After our last trip to the States for a much-needed rest, we were soon faced with another problem. We had to renew our visas. How could this be done without a sponsoring organization in the States? When filling out the application, I could only put down that I was sponsoring myself, and that I would guarantee the payment of all bills. I also put myself as Mom's sponsor and turned the papers in to see what would happen. We were sure that only God could make this work. It would be several days before we would know. The Vietnamese were very slow and deliberate about such matters. At the appointed date, we were back to see what the verdict would be. We knew that only the Lord could make it possible for such an application to be accepted. It was! This was another evidence of God's favor upon our work.

Soon we were faced with another situation with the military. To get our identification cards renewed, which would permit us to have access to military instillations, it was becoming very difficult for civilians working in this country. If one was not working for some company that was under contract with our government, it was just about an impossibility. Only God could cut through the red tape and enable us to get through, and He did! Even a chaplain, who was a colonel, told us that according to the latest regulations, it would seem utterly impossible for us to obtain ID cards. Again, we could only trust the Lord.

Just about everything depended on our having these ID cards. One thing that was very important to us was the postal privilege. Had we been forced to use the international mail service; it would have been a great hindrance to our work. There would have been many other ways in which our work would have been hindered. But God answered our prayer and that which was seemingly impossible, according to military regulations, was done.

God began to open doors for us to speak to some of the Vietnamese churches. There was a hunger for the moving of the Holy Spirit in their lives. This came about through some English-speaking Vietnamese servicemen who had attended our meetings. They enjoyed the freedom and joy that was manifested in our worship services as a result of this. We were soon being invited to speak in several of their churches. They would request that we speak to them about the work of the Holy Spirit in the life of the believer.

A Buddhist monk came to the center one day. He could speak good English. We witnessed to him about the saving grace of Jesus Christ. He later came to one of our meetings and then invited us to come to their university and speak to a class of forty monks. He requested that we speak to them about the Holy Spirit. We presented God's plan of salvation, through faith in Jesus Christ, and His promise of the Holy Spirit to all who would believe. We did pray the message would yet bear fruit in that they would accept Jesus as Savior.

The leading of the Lord was so precious although hard to understand. We reached a place where our ministry was in the center and the hospitals were enabling us to reach more with the gospel, and the financial support was becoming sufficient to meet every need. It was then that we began to feel that we should return to the States.

Returning to the States would present a new challenge to us. We would have no home to go to, and as far as we knew, we would have no ministry, and we would have no support. This would be another step of faith.

It was not easy for us to come to the place where we could look for someone to take over the center. We knew the work must continue as long as American servicemen were in Vietnam. Just who would be willing to come to such a place? Just who would have the burden for such a work? In due time a young couple was found that would be willing to come to Vietnam and take over the center.

We were soon making plans to return to the States by way of Europe. We had a desire to visit the Holy Land and minister in a few places on the way home. From Tel Aviv, we flew to Frankfurt, Germany, and then by train to Kaiserslautern where we were guests of Chaplain Major Hunt. We were permitted to speak in several military chapels and met several of the servicemen that had been with us in Vietnam.

From Germany, we flew to London and then to New York. It seemed good to be back in the States again. We would never forget the miracles of God during these five years in Vietnam.

# Epilogue

Mom and Pop were blessed to be asked to again minister in the church in Garfield, Washington. This was their home until 1983. At this time, Mom suffered a stroke, and they decided to move to Oak Harbor, Washington, where their eldest daughter and husband resided and pastored a church. Mom passed in 1986 and Pop in 1991. They so enjoyed the visits, calls, and letters from servicemen who had become so special to them during their ministry in Vietnam.

As we relate our stories of God's marvelous work in our lives, it can only bring encouragement and blessing to others. It is so important to impart to those around us that the God of the Bible is still at work today. Stories are powerful and can change lives. If Christ Jesus is in your story, you have a powerful story. Our parents, Mom and Pop Kincaid, seemed somewhat reluctant to tell their story as they never wanted attention given to themselves but only to let others know the power of God in working miracles and answering prayers.

To all the servicemen and servicewomen who have served our country, we say thank you. A special thanks to Roderick and Vickie for being such a blessing and help to Mom and Pop.

I received an email from Roderick in 2017.

> Pop Kincaid flew on gunships all over the 3 Corps area visiting the wounded and dying in every field hospital. For six years he did this, no breaks, day in and day out risking his life along with our troops. He was in an ongoing successive

rapport with chaplains each year, they rotated and left behind them the word to their successors that Rev. Kincaid was a man of God of the highest character to be entrusted with sharing the pastoral care of the suffering and dying! This servant of God sought only to glorify God and help his fellow men with prayer and the saving message of the Gospel! I personally witnessed this humble servant's ministry, first as a trouper and later as a lay volunteer!

Also, George and Liz Greenwood for encouraging the Kincaid family to make the story of Mom and Pop available and hopefully a blessing to someone. Roderick and George, you both have stories to tell of how God mightily kept you safe and blessed you while serving your country in Vietnam.

Nora Kincaid Pinter, daughter of Mom and Pop.

JOURNEY OF FAITH

## Introducing Mom and Pop Kincaid...

More than twenty months ago, Mom and I started the first Christian Servicemen's Center in Viet Nam. This is also the first and still the only FULL GOSPEL work in South Viet Nam.

When we came here the Buddhists were demonstrating, and there were mines being planted in various places in the City of Saigon. One was never sure about their being safe on the streets. But it is so much different now. One is able to move about with very little fear.

Reverend Eddie Karnes visited Saigon in the fall of 1966. He saw that there was no place for the service men to go during their off duty hours, but the bars. He knew there should to be a servicemen's center in the City of Saigon. He wondered who would be willing to come over into this troubled city and open up a center. On his return to the States, he wrote us about the need, and asked if we would consider going. After prayer, we knew that the Lord had already prepared our hearts for this job.

This was an entirely new venture of faith for us. We felt the urge to get on the field as soon as possible, so we only took one month to itinerate.

Mom & Pop Kincaid, Saigon, Viet Nam

We were only able to visit a few churches, and to acquaint a few of our friends with the work we planned to do.

During the past twenty months, we have seen God do some very wonderful things in the hearts of the service men. One very happy mother and father wrote us recently, 'You have made a deep impression on our son John and he is still interested in becoming a minister. -- He will be leaving the service about the end of February and then plans to finish his schooling for the ministry.'

Only eternity will reveal what this ministry will mean to the souls of the service men. We thank God for the little part we have in it.

*Mom & Pop Kincaid*

**FEBRUARY 1968** *article from World Harvest magazine*

# 1971

**SAIGON CHRISTIAN SERVICEMEN'S CENTER**
Hem 36/253/5A Cach-Mang
(One block behind the CARLTON HOTEL)
CMR Box 3552, APO S/F Calif. 96201
Phone MACV 3203

**GOOD NEWS PUBLISHERS • Westchester, Illinois 60153**

## All this can be yours...

**FORGIVENESS**
'For in Christ our release is secured and our sins are forgiven through the shedding of His blood.'  Ephesians 1:7

**SALVATION**
Only in Christ, 'for there is no other name under heaven granted to men by which we may receive salvation.'  Acts 4:12b

**LIFE FOREVER**
'God has given us eternal life, and...this life is found in His Son,' Jesus Christ.  I John 5:12

**PEACE**
'Now that we have been justified through faith, we are at peace with God through our Lord Jesus Christ.'  Romans 5:1

## ...if you'll believe today

Scripture quotations are from the New English Bible • Printed in the U.S.A.

# JOURNEY OF FAITH

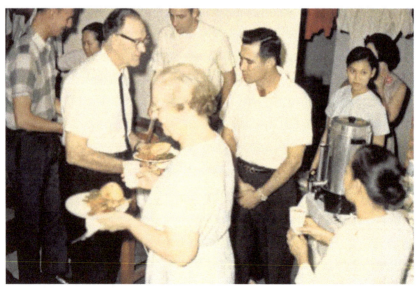

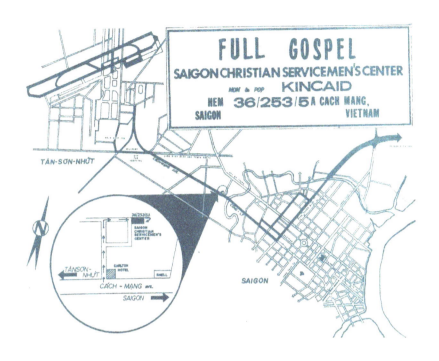

MOM AND POP KINCAID, FOUNDERS OF THE SAIGON CHRISTIAN SERVICEMEN'S CENTER

THESE FAITH MISSIONARIES LIVED THRU THE RECENT COMMUNIST KILLINGS OF SIX AMERICAN MISSIONARIES IN VIETNAM. WITH POSSIBLE DANGERS AHEAD MOM AND POP KINCAID ARE PREPARING TO RETURN TO VIETNAM FOR A SECOND TOUR OF DUTY FOR TWO O YEARS ON MAY 20TH. THEY NEED YOUR HELP TO KEEP THE DOORS OF HAPPINESS OPEN AT THE SAIGON CHRISTIAN SERVICEMEN'S CENTER. THE RENT IS $400 A MONTH.

THE SAIGON CHRISTIAN SERVICEMEN'S CENTER

POP KINCAID IN VIETNAM WITH BILLY GRAHAM

OUR SIGN JUST OFF SAIGON'S BUSIEST ROAD

VIETNAM SUPPER TIME WITH MOM AND POP KINCAID

A GI REACHING A BUDDY FOR CHRIST WITH A TRACT   POP KINCAID BUSY IN HOSPITAL EVANGELISM

# JOURNEY OF FAITH

THE WHITE HOUSE

WASHINGTON

September 19, 1983

Dear Mr. and Mrs. Kincaid:

Someone who admires you very much has told me of the wonderful contributions you made on behalf of our servicemen in Saigon during the Vietnam War. Stories like yours only reaffirm my faith in the goodness of man. Your special calling and your willingness to make a home away from home for the many people who crossed your threshold has earned you not only the love of those you assisted, but their undying gratitude as well. Our nation is enhanced because of your shining example.

Mrs. Kincaid, I was very sorry to learn of your illness. Nancy joins me in sending our best wishes and prayers for easier days ahead for you.

God bless you both for the service you have performed in His name.

With warm regards,

Sincerely,

*Ronald Reagan*

Reverend and Mrs. Wade A. Kincaid

# JOURNEY OF FAITH

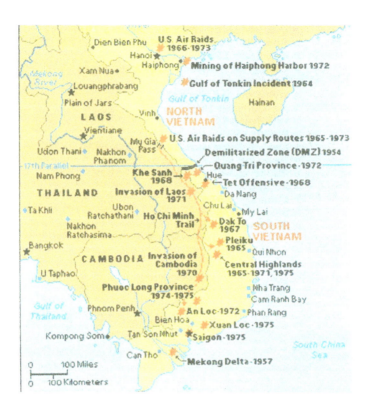

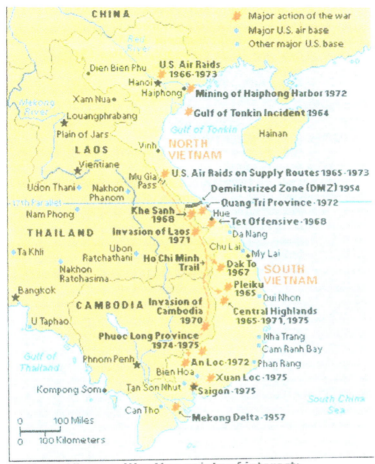

Major Vietnam War Map points of interest:

> Mekong Delta 1957 U.S Air Raids 1966-1973
> Mining of Haiphong Harbour 1964
> Gulf of Tonkin Incident 1964
> U.S. Air Raids on Supply Routes 1965-1973
> Demilitarized Zone (DMZ) 1954

# JOURNEY OF FAITH

## Pop and Mom Kincaid

**Kincaids visit grandchildren after five years in Saigon**

A visit with the grandchildren proves to be a special treat for the Rev. and Mrs. W. A. (Mom and Pop) Kincaid. This holiday season was the first one at home for the Kincaids in five years. The Kincaids have returned to Garfield after serving at the Saigon Servicemen's Center since 1966. Visiting their grandparents, from the left, are Dianne 11, Linda 10, and Debbie 8 daughters of Mr. and Mrs. Leonard Pinter of Belmont. Randy Pinter, 13, was unable to be present when the picture was taken. The girls was holding Vietnam dolls which were presented to the Kincaids by the Saigon landlord.

# JOURNEY OF FAITH

Guess whom!
Shopping with a Vietnamese one.
A tea set at left hand for my
mother and a glass of flowers at
Right hand for my dear Mom
Kincaid — With love —

Pop and Mom would surely like to share this booklet/tract, which they had given by the many thousands, in this Journey of Faith.

# Here's How!

*A fascinating short story involving the greatest issue of all time...*

THEY met while flying westward across the nation—two young men, Dr. Westman and Jack Strong. They became fast friends when they discovered they were graduates of the same university. After an interesting conversation about their school a serious discussion arose. It all began when the doctor, after a pause in the conversation, remarked, "We live in terrible times, Jack. Are you ready for what's ahead?"

"I'm not worried about what's ahead," Jack laughed. "I believe this old world has a glorious future."

"Listen, Jack," the doctor returned, "prophecies throughout the Bible predict that this age is going to wind up in such a terrible time of tribulation and war and bloodshed that it will be multiplied times worse than anything that has ever happened in the history of man.

"Part of the end time prophecy predicts that one-third of the people on earth will be killed in a matter of a few months. The earth has a population of almost five billion people, which means that some 1,666,000,000 (1,666

*Page One*

million) people will be killed in that period alone—not to mention all the rest of the bloodshed and horror predicted for the end. The 23,000,000 (23 million) soldiers and civilians over the world who died from all causes of World War II will be a mere drop in the bucket in comparison.

"There are many end time prophecies about Israel and other nations which are being fulfilled right now. This is no time to refuse to be concerned, and to shut our eyes to the prophecies in the Bible about the last days. *We are living right now in the last days!* It's time to be concerned about being prepared to meet God at any moment!"

"Why do we need to be prepared to meet God?" Jack questioned. "I have no fear nor concern about meeting God."

"You should have concern! We will all stand before God for judgment. As Creator, as the greatest Power, the greatest Intelligence, and as Possessor of the highest moral character in existence it is both God's right and His duty to govern the universe. We are all under obligation to obey the commands of God. And no law is of any consequence if there is not a penalty for every act of disobedience. God says, 'It is appointed unto men once to die, but after this the judgment.'

"The apostle Paul said, in the book of Romans in the Bible, chapter 14, verse 12,

*Page Two*

'Every one of us shall give account of himself to God.' Jesus Christ taught that every word and act of all persons would come up for judgment. Matthew 12:36 records that Christ said, 'Every idle word that men shall speak, they shall give account thereof in the day of judgment.' "

"I don't believe that God is keeping a record of everything we do," Jack broke in.

"Look at this then," the doctor answered as he took his Bible from his brief case. "Listen to what it says here in Proverbs 15:3, 'The eyes of the Lord are in every place, beholding the evil and the good.'

"Then look back here in Revelation, chapter 20, beginning with verse 12. 'And I saw the dead, small and great, stand before God; and the books were opened: and another book was opened, which is the book of life: and the dead were judged out of those things which were written in the books, according to their works. And the sea gave up the dead which were in it; and death and hell delivered up the dead which were in them: and they were judged every man according to their works. And death and hell were cast into the lake of fire. This is the second death. And whosoever was not found written in the book of life was cast into the lake of fire.' So you see God is keeping a complete record of every one of us."

"Well, maybe," Jack answered, "but it says

*Page Three*

there that everyone will be judged according to his works. So, if my good deeds outweigh my evil deeds I'll make out all right."

"Jack, if you had faithfully obeyed the laws of the state up to this time, and then today you killed a man, would the state endeavor to find out if your good deeds outweighed this evil deed, or would you be punished for your crime without consideration being given to your past life?"

"I'd be punished. But that's entirely different."

"Not at all. The state expects you to live right, and you are punished if you don't. God also expects you to live right, and when you fail to obey the moral law of what is right, and when you disobey God's definite commands, you face judgment by God."

"Well, even if you should be right about that, who really knows how to be prepared to meet God? Some people think they know, but I'll be honest enough to admit that I don't know—and I don't believe anyone else knows for sure either. What's more, I'm really not much concerned. I belong to church and try to live a respectable life. Here's the way I look at it—If I live a respectable life and treat my fellow-men right, and if I pay my debts, I'll make out all right. God won't hold anything against me if I do the best I can. He won't expect me to do better than my best. That's my religion, and I think

*Page Four*

it's a pretty good religion."

"Jack, you said you believe that if you did your best you would be ready to meet God. Let me ask you—Are you doing your best?"

"Well, I suppose there are times when I could do better."

"If you could do better you are not doing your best, so you are lost even according to your own religion. The Bible says, 'All have sinned,' and, 'The wages of sin is death.'"

"I'm not a sinner!" Jack interrupted. "I've always lived a respectable life."

"Jesus said that a sinful thought was just as wrong as a sinful act. When an evil thought comes into our minds, and we don't put it out the moment we are conscious of it, we are guilty in God's sight of committing the very act of sin we allowed ourselves to think about. Every one of us has sinned, and we all stand condemned before God unless we have found the one and only way to have our guilt removed."

"What do you mean?" Jack questioned. "Even if we could have all guilt removed we wouldn't be able to know it."

"You're in the same place I was, Jack, but a friend of mine showed me some remarkable things concerning life and the hereafter. I'd like to show you the things this friend showed me; how we can *know* what the outcome of our meeting with God will be."

*Page Five*

"How can you be so sure that you know?"

In a firm but kind voice the doctor answered, "I know I've found the truth, and I'm sure you'll agree when you hear how simple and plain and wonderful the truth is. In your present state you are a condemned sinner, which is a terrible condition for anyone to be in. But I can show you how you can receive eternal life instead, and know it."

"All right," Jack agreed, "let's hear it anyway. I can't lose anything by it."

"Let me start by asking you a question. If you were God, what would you do? Just suppose that here you are—you're God—there's nothing but you to begin with. You have infinite power and wisdom. You can do whatever you desire. What would you do?"

"I suppose I'd make some worlds and suns and moons," Jack answered with a grin.

"Why?"

"I don't know. Why did God make them?"

"He made them because He had a need. God never does anything without good reason."

Jack thought a moment, and then said, "The only problem I can see that God might have had when He was all alone would have been that with all that empty space, and without anyone else around, He must have had a very desolate and lonely existence."

"You're right! That was God's need—He needed someone to love, and someone who

*Page Six*

would love Him. The Bible says, 'God is love.' His very essence is love. The main driving force within Him is love. There is so much in the Bible about God's love. In fact, the whole Bible is actually a love story—recording the various ramifications of God's dealings with men as He seeks to woo them—using both pain and blessing to bring us to Himself.

"And the only beings that could really love God to His complete satisfaction would be beings like Himself. God loves the birds and animals, but not nearly with the intensity that He loves the sons He has created in His own image and likeness. Genesis, the first book in the Bible, records that God created the earth and the entire universe. Then after bringing forth vegetation and animal life on the earth God said, as recorded in Genesis 1:26, 'Let us make man in our image, after our likeness.'"

"Say, I read that once," Jack interrupted. "That doesn't make sense. If God was the Creator of everything, to whom was He talking there?"

"The answer to that is found in the New Testament, in Hebrews 1:2. Let's read it here. 'God hath in these last days spoken unto us by His Son, whom He hath appointed heir of all things, by whom also He made the worlds.' It says there that God created the worlds through His Son. He was speaking

*Page Seven*

to His Son and to the Holy Spirit when He said, 'Let us make man in our image.' "

"You said something a moment ago," Jack spoke up, "about God creating sons in His own image and likeness, who would give Him the love He so greatly desired. Did He create the Son you speak of here sometime before He created these other sons?"

"No, the Son of God, mentioned here in Hebrews 1:2 and in many other places in the Bible, was not created. He was begotten, or born of the Father. As one of the confessions of faith states, He was "begotten, not made.' "

"Well, how do you explain that?"

Shaking his head, the doctor answered, "What took place in eternity before the universe was created is something that God has not chosen to reveal to us. However, God *has* revealed to us that He has a begotten Son, and that this Son is our Creator. Therefore, His Son is also God. Then just think what it implied when God said, 'Let us make man in our image, after our likeness.' In creating us in His own image and likeness God has given us a possible future which is absolutely astounding! But notice what happened.

"Adam and Eve, the first man and woman God created, were placed in a beautiful garden called Eden. They had wonderful fellowship with God there. God visited them, and

*Page Eight*

walked and talked with them. But just the same Adam and Eve rebelled against Him. And they were banished by God from this paradise for their disobedience and rebellion. Being created in the image of God, man has the power of choice. God was testing Adam and Eve—and they failed the test!

"They failed to appreciate their true relationship to God—that He was their Father, who loved them dearly. They didn't understand that it was God's great love that had motivated Him to create them. They thought only about satisfying their own lusts and desires instead of seeking to bring joy to their wonderful God and Father.

"When creating us in His own image and likeness God put within each one of us the same deep need for love that was within Him. And this need within each of us can only be fully met and completely satisfied when we say an unconditional 'yes' to God, and accept His love as our complete fulfillment for life and eternity. There's an emptiness within each of us that only God can fill!

"We sometimes criticize Adam for disobeying God, but every one of us has spurned God's love, and we've tried to satisfy the craving within us by satisfying the lusts of our body and mind. We have all rebelled against God. We have all gone our own way. Psalm 14:2 and 3 says, 'The Lord looked down from heaven upon the children of men

*Page Nine*

to see if there were any that did understand, and seek God. They are all gone aside, they are all together become filthy: there is none that doeth good, no, not one.'

"The Hebrew word translated 'understand' in the scripture I just read means to 'act with understanding and intelligence.' Until God took the initiative to reach out and rescue us, none of us acted with understanding and intelligence toward Him. We've all gone our own filthy ways. And Ezekiel 18:20 says, 'The soul that sinneth, it shall die!'

"We find then that even though we have been created in the image of God, and our heritage could have been a glorious heritage with God as His sons, we have all rebelled and we are all under the sentence of death. And this death is more than mere physical death. It will be the second death that we just read about. Death means separation. Physical death takes place when the soul is separated from the body. The second death will occur when the soul is separated from, or banished from God, in the lake of fire."

"That's another thing I can't understand," Jack interrupted. "If God is the God of love that you say He is, where do folks get the idea that He will punish anyone in Hell?"

"You can be *sure* that you will be punished in Hell," the doctor answered, "unless you repent of your sins, and unless the guilt of your sin is removed, because God says so in

*Page Ten*

the Bible time after time. Whatever God says —positively will happen! He has absolutely no choice—He must punish the sinner! If His nature were such that He had to forgive if we simply asked His forgiveness, His entire Kingdom would crumble. The vilest sinners could then simply ask His forgiveness whenever they were brought up for judgment, and upon receiving His forgiveness they could go right back to their sinning, because they could get by again and again merely by asking forgiveness. The same would apply to the Devil. Terrifying anarchy would prevail.

"Also God is altogether holy and righteous. He would not continue to be holy and righteous if He did not judge sin, because by His very laxness and indifference He would be party to the sin and rebellion He allowed. If God failed to judge sin He would be *permitting* rebellion against righteousness, thereby legalizing lawlessness and anarchy, and giving license and liberty to our lusts and passions, instead of righteously making us responsible to obey Him and do what is right.

"God's very nature of absolute holiness and righteousness *impels* Him to judge and punish sin. Therefore, in your unforgiven state you are hopelessly lost, and doomed to exile in Hell, unless you can somehow be pardoned!"

"I never thought of God's nature and character entering into the matter," Jack

*Page Eleven*

admitted, "But say, I was just thinking, you stated that our guilt can be removed. If that happens are we then restored to favor with God, and to our position as His sons?"

"Yes. But you're getting ahead of me. Let me explain. God positively cannot and will not tolerate rebellion and disobedience. He has therefore decreed that every sinner shall appear before Him for judgment. But God's nature is also dominated by love, which *impelled* Him to find a way by which He could offer pardon for our sins. 'He is not willing that any should perish.' However, in order to offer us pardon there had to be a way found by which God could judge sin—and at the same time make it possible for Him to save the sinner. That sounds like an impossible thing to do—but God found a way. The Bible clearly teaches that God foresaw the fall of man even before the earth was formed, and that He had also determined at that time what He would do, so that He could offer forgiveness.

"Throughout the Old Testament God continually foretold through His prophets the coming of a great Savior of the world. The 53rd chapter of Isaiah even foretold *how* the Savior would redeem us.

"In Isaiah 7:14 we find this prophecy concerning the Savior, 'The Lord Himself shall give you a sign. Behold, a virgin shall conceive, and bear a son, and shall call

*Page Twelve*

His name Immanuel,' The name Immanuel means, 'God with us.'

"Then also in Isaiah 9:6 we read about Him. Let's read it from the Bible. Here it is: 'For unto us a child is born, unto us a Son is given; and the government shall be upon His shoulder: and His name shall be called Wonderful, Counsellor, The Mighty God, The Everlasting Father, The Prince of Peace.' "

"Say, it sounds as if He's God too," Jack interrupted. "What's the meaning of that?"

"It's just this, Jack: It was determined in the councils of God before the earth was formed that the Son of God who created us would also make the way possible for God to forgive our sins. The Son of God, our Creator, took upon Himself a body like our own and became a man. He was born of a virgin, the virgin Mary, just as God foretold. He had no earthly father. His father was God.

"Our Savior is none other than Jesus Christ. In many ways He manifested the fact that He was the Son of God—by His miracles, the greatest miracle being when He arose from the dead, by the words He spoke, and possibly most of all by the perfect and sinless life He lived. The apostle Peter wrote concerning Him, in these words, 'Who did no sin, neither was guile found in His mouth.' The apostle John said concerning His sinlessness, 'And ye know how He was mani-

*Page Thirteen*

fested to take away our sins, and in Him is no sin.' Jack, Christ was the first and only man who ever lived without sin. He lived the only perfect life ever lived. If that's the case, here was one man who was not under the sentence of death for sin, not even physical death. But He did die, didn't He?"

"Yes, that's what I've heard."

"Why did He die, Jack? The answer is—He came to this earth for the express purpose of suffering and pouring out His life's blood for us—because of our sins. By His sacrifice for us, and by His resurrection from the dead —gaining VICTORY over sin and death—He became THE WAY through whom we can be redeemed and pardoned by God.

"As you no doubt know, Jesus Christ was hated and despised for the truth He spoke and lived. Finally, He was beaten and nailed to a wooden cross, on which He died. God allowed this to happen to Christ. In fact, that was the plan. God JUDGED sin by offering His Son, in whom there was no sin, as a sacrifice for sin! The prophet Isaiah prophesied. 'The Lord hath laid on Him (on Christ) the iniquity of us all.' Isaiah also prophesied, 'He was wounded for our transgressions, He was bruised for our iniquities: the chastisement of our peace was upon Him; and with His stripes we are healed.' The main theme of the Bible is—*Salvation through Jesus Christ!*"

*Page Fourteen*

"Well, just what did Christ's death on the cross accomplish?" Jack questioned. "I mean —How can His death be the means of removing the sin in my life?"

"It's like this," the doctor answered, "God placed all sin upon Christ, including your sin and mine. It seems that God considered Christ on the cross as SIN PERSONIFIED, because the Bible says, 'He became sin for us.' JUDGMENT was poured out upon sin on the cross! God sacrificed Christ on the cross as a sin offering for the sins of the whole world. Up to this time God had directed that various animals were to be sacrificed for sin, but these animal sacrifices merely pictured the great sacrifice for sin which God would give. When Christ walked on earth John the Baptist pointed to Christ and prophesied, under the inspiration of God, 'Behold the Lamb of God, which taketh away the sin of the world!' There is now no more need for animal sacrifices. God now offers us pardon for our sins because of the sacrifice of Christ on the cross for us. He paid the redemption price with His own blood. He suffered for you, for your sins and mine. Peter said, 'Ye were not redeemed with corruptible things, as silver and gold...but with the precious blood of Christ.'

"I can't explain in just a few minutes all that is involved in Christ's death for us. In fact, no mortal man fully understands what

*Page Fifteen*

God in His wisdom has done for us through Christ. But we do know that God's Word says that 'God so loved the world, that He gave His only begotten Son, that whosoever believeth in Him should not perish, but have everlasting life.'

"No one can explain what electricity is, but we use it. We have eternal life offered us through Christ, and through Him alone. We must use the means God has provided, even if we cannot fully understand it, or we are forever lost! Christ said, 'I am the way, the truth, and the life; no man cometh unto the Father, but by me.' There is absolutely no other way. God will recognize no other way—no matter how logical it may seem—and no matter how sincere a person may be. Until one recognizes and accepts the sacrifice of Christ on the cross as the sin offering for his sins, he is still lost!

"Paul the apostle states, in Colossians 1:13, 14, 'God hath delivered us from the power of darkness, and hath translated us into the kingdom of His dear Son: in whom we have redemption through His blood, even the forgiveness of sins.' "

"Can everyone receive God's forgiveness now," Jack asked, "by simply asking forgiveness?"

"Anyone can now receive forgiveness from God, if he is willing to fulfill the conditions required for forgiveness."

*Page Sixteen*

"What conditions do you mean?"

"It would be wrong for God to forgive anyone whose mind was still set in rebellion against Him," the doctor answered. "No honest civil government would pardon a criminal if they knew that in his mind he planned to continue in his old life of crime. The only conditions upon which God can righteously forgive any sinner is if the supreme desire of that person has changed from selfish, self-centered, self-willed indulgence to a supreme desire to live in full obedience to God.

"The apostle Peter said, 'Repent ye, therefore, and be converted that your sins may be blotted out.' That's the condition God lays down. The prescription for eternal life is *'repentance* toward God, and *faith* toward the Lord Jesus Christ' as recorded in Acts 20:21. The word repent means to have a changed mind, or a changed heart.

"Throughout the Bible you will find God dealing with men about the condition of their hearts. God is not speaking here of the physical heart in the human body. He is speaking about the very governing center of your being—the heart center where your supreme desires and affections are rooted.

"Our desires and affections have produced sin and rebellion against God and righteousness. God testifies to the fact that we all 'have turned everyone to his own way.' To

*Page Seventeen*

repent means to consciously and definitely *turn* from our selfish, self-centered, self-willed way, to unconditional surrender to God—asking *Him* to rule in our hearts, and purposing that the supreme and ruling desire of our hearts shall henceforth be to please Him in all things.

"Christ called this change of heart being 'born again.' He said to a Jewish leader named Nicodemus, 'Except a man be born again, he cannot see the kingdom of God.' Later on He said to the same man, 'Ye *must* be born again.' Notice the emphasis Christ gave to this truth."

"I don't believe I could hold out," Jack responded.

"Jack, when a person has a *change of heart* toward God, and trusts in Christ as his Savior—something wonderful happens. It's this: God actually enters the heart and life of that person to reign there. He is also there to *help* that person in his living.

"This is another mystery which cannot be explained in the natural. However in John 14:23 we read that Christ said, 'If a person really loves me he will obey my words. Then my Father will love him, and we will come to him and will make our home with him.' In Revelation 3:20 and 21 Christ is shown knocking at the door of man's heart, and He says, 'Behold, I stand at the door and knock: if any man hear my voice, and open the door,

*Page Eighteen*

I will come in to him, and will sup with him, and he with me. To him that overcometh will I grant to sit with me in my throne, even as I also overcame, and am set down with my Father in his throne.'

"Christ will help you to overcome. He knows better than you do that even as a Christian you cannot overcome temptation and sin without His help. I Corinthians 10:13 states, 'God is faithful, who will not suffer you to be tempted above that ye are able; but will with the temptation also make a way to escape, that ye may be able to bear it.' Then also, Philippians 2:13 states, 'It is God which worketh in you both to will and to do of His good pleasure.' "

"Do you mean that God does everything for us?" Jack questioned.

"No, God will never tamper with your power of choice. The actual decisions are your responsibility. God is even now knocking at your heart's door, convicting you of your lost condition, but He will never *force* you to give Him entrance. Also, even though God works in a Christian 'to will and to do of His good pleasure,' He does not force His will even there.

"Even a Christian is tempted by Satan to do evil. One of Satan's prime areas of attack is in our thought life. But our Lord has commanded us, 'Resist the Devil and he will flee from you.' But then the question follows,

*Page Nineteen*

'How do we resist him? How can we resist him when he is so much stronger than we?' The answer is that Jesus gained victory over Satan for us when He was crucified on the cross for our sins. Satan is a defeated foe! He now must obey the true Christian when he *resists* him by command.

"What I do, personally, and what many others do, is to command Satan in the name of Jesus Christ. Usually when an evil thought comes into my mind, I put it away and think of something else. But if the thought keeps coming back I realize that I need help. Therefore, I resist Satan by saying to him, 'Satan, I command you in the name of Jesus Christ my Savior, *leave me and stop tempting me!*' And it works!

"A Christian has temptations and decisions which must be met daily. But with God's help—and with a new mind and heart with desires and affections that are toward Christ instead of self—we can overcome victoriously. And if we should stumble and sin, we have the loving promise in I John 1:9 that 'If we confess our sins, He is faithful and just to forgive us our sins, and to cleanse us from all unrighteousness.'

"However, one cannot take this promise of forgiveness as meaning that a Christian can live his life just as he chooses, and be forgiven whenever he chooses. A person who reasons this way is not a Christian. John

*Page Twenty*

warns about this a few verses further on, as you see here, 'And hereby we do know that we know Him, if we keep His commandments. He that saith, I know Him (or, I'm a Christian) and keepeth not His commandments, is a liar, and the truth is not in him. But whoso keepeth His word, in him verily is the love of God perfected: hereby know we that we are in Him.' "

"Well," Jack again spoke up, "I know several folk who are supposed to be very sincere Christians, but they are just as self-centered and self-seeking as anyone else."

"Jack, look at this passage in Matthew 7:21-23, 'Not every one that saith unto me, Lord, Lord, shall enter into the kingdom of Heaven; but he that doeth the will of my Father which is in Heaven. Many will say to me in that day, Lord, Lord, have we not prophesied in thy name?...and in thy name have done many wonderful works? And then will I profess unto them, I never knew you: depart from me, ye that work iniquity.'

"It's a sobering thing, Jack, to realize that the Lord warns here that there will be *many* who think they are right with God who will discover that they never did have a real change of heart. And they will be lost! Paul says in II Corinthians 5:17, 'Therefore if any man be in Christ, he is a new creature: old things are passed away; behold, all things are become new.' A person who becomes a

*Page Twenty-one*

Christian becomes a new person. He no longer lives to please self—but God.

"Do you know others who profess to be Christians who really live it?"

"Yes," Jack replied thoughtfully, "I surely do. If I'm ever going to be a Christian I'm going to be like them."

"Right now is the time to make your decision on this, Jack. 'Repentance toward God, and faith toward our Lord Jesus Christ' is what God requires. If you recognize and believe the fact that Jesus Christ died for your sins, the only other thing that remains on your part is to turn from your self-will in submission to God's will, and receive Christ as Savior and Lord of your life.

"Look what God says here in Ezekiel 18:31, 32, 'Cast away from you all your transgressions, whereby ye have transgressed; and make you a new heart and a new spirit: for why will ye die...? For I have no pleasure in the death of him that dieth, saith the Lord: wherefore turn yourselves, and live ye.' The moment you truly do that in your mind and heart God will forgive. Repentance and all that it means, on your part, and forgiveness, on God's part, happen at the same moment. God stands ready to forgive the moment you truly repent. God's offer of forgiveness is yours today. It may be too late tomorrow, or even an hour from now."

"I don't believe I'm quite ready just yet,"

*Page Twenty-two*

Jack replied.

"Do you mean that even when you understand the way to eternal life, that you are actually telling God that you would rather remain a condemned sinner than to receive His pardon?"

"I don't mean that," Jack answered. "I just don't feel in the mood for making such a decision just now."

"You have your chance *now* to receive eternal life, Jack. Suppose that God should decide that you have had all the opportunity you need, and should take you from this life before another day dawns. It's utterly foolish to put off such an important decision for even one hour."

After some moments of silence, Jack answered, "It will cost me too much."

"It will cost you too much not to obtain God's forgiveness," Dr. Westman answered. "Think of the cost of judgment in Hell! Is anything worth going to Hell for?"

"No."

"Then make the right decision. This is a matter of life or death! Life in this world is becoming more uncertain every day, and it's foolish to put off such an important decision! Is any cost too great if it means getting right with God and obtaining everlasting life? 'What shall it profit a man if he shall gain the whole world, and lose his own soul'?

"You stand condemned already until you

*Page Twenty-three*

turn from your sins in surrender to God. Each hour you live will bring you that much nearer the bar of God's justice."

After another moment of careful thought, Jack answered, "I know you're right." There was another pause. Then Jack stated, "I really do want to get right with God. I realize it's the only thing that really counts."

"Be sure you fully count the cost, Jack. If you mean business with God, fine. But if you don't really mean business—remember, you can't fool God. God must have all—or nothing! God will not pardon and give you peace of mind unless you truly yield your will to Him."

"I mean business."

"If you really do, let's tell God about it right now."

The doctor prayed first, and then, Jack, in a short prayer told God what was on his heart.

As Jack finished he sat in silent thought. Finally he turned to Dr. Westman and said, "I don't think it will do any good."

"It will be your fault if it doesn't do any good, Jack. The apostle Paul said, 'Christ Jesus came into the world to save sinners; of whom I am chief.' If God would forgive the chief of sinners, He will forgive anyone else. What are you holding back from God, Jack? No, it won't do any good unless you surrender that thing that God is allowing the

*Page Twenty-four*

Devil to test you with right now. Surrender that along with the rest and God will forgive and give you peace and joy."

Jack sat in silence for several minutes. Finally the doctor spoke. "Just talk to the Lord about it, Jack. God wants to help you even concerning the testing that's before you now."

Jack turned slightly toward the window, and with his elbow on the armrest he bowed his head in his hand. A struggle was ensuing in Jack's burdened heart as the Spirit of God sought to dethrone self and enthrone God there. The Spirit of God wrestles in such moments to give birth to a new life. After several minutes Jack wiped a tear from each eye with his handkerchief. Decisions and surrenders of eternal importance were being made in those solemn moments. After several more minutes Jack again used his handkerchief. Then he turned to the doctor, and with moist eyes, in glistening, grim determination stated, "It's all settled, Doc. From now on, I'm on God's side. Whatever He says goes." As he spoke, the words seemed to release all the burdens of his heart. Grimness gave place to the sunrise of a smile which quickly spread over his entire face, as the two men grasped each other's hand.

"It's as if a big load had been lifted from me," Jack spoke again, with deep emotion. "I wish I could tell others about it in the

*Page Twenty-five*

same way that you've told me. Life doesn't have much meaning without the certainty of a happy future. I've been forcing myself to believe that everything would turn out all right. But now I know I was wrong. I'm certainly grateful to you for showing me the truth, and for convincing me to face the issue NOW. Everyone should be told this wonderful news!"

Dr. Westman was thrilled with the joy which only a winner of souls can experience. "That's exactly what the Lord wants you to do!" he exclaimed. "Christ's great commission to us is recorded in Mark 16:15, 'Go ye into all the world, and preach the gospel to every creature.'

"The thing for you to do, Jack, is to immediately search out a real Bible-believing and Christ-loving church in your town, get baptized there and get busy with them in winning others. Make friends of Christians who really mean business, and serve the Lord together with them. In the book of Daniel we have the promise that 'They that turn many to righteousness shall shine as the stars forever.' I don't know what that shining means, but you can be sure that it will be something of *great* value.

"Christ commanded that every one who trusted in Him for salvation should be baptized. So, be sure that you obey your Lord in this as well as in all other things."

*Page Twenty-six*

"Dr. Westman," Jack again spoke, "I can never repay you for showing me the way to everlasting life, but I hope I can be the means of doing for others what you've done for me."

The doctor smiled as he saw the set determination in Jack's face and eyes. "That's proof enough for me that you've really come through for the Lord," he answered. "My prayer for you is that God will use you as a fearless weapon in His hand.

"God bless you, Jack."

\* \* \* \*

Listen, friend, you too are lost unless you have come to God for forgiveness of your sin through Jesus Christ, and unless you have been genuinely born again.

It isn't enough merely to know and believe these facts about salvation through Christ. "You must be born again." And that new birth must be manifested by a changed life resulting from a changed mind and heart.

God loves you and wants to save you. Undoubtedly He has arranged circumstances so that you would read this little booklet, that He might show you your hopeless, lost condition, and then show you how you may receive His pardon. God says in the book of Hebrews that to refuse the truth and spurn His love means for that person "a *certain,* fearful looking for of judgment and fiery indignation." God has here shown you the way by which you can be pardoned. There is no

*Page Twenty-seven*

other way. You may receive life *on His terms* —otherwise forget about Heaven, and face the fact that *you have chosen* to continue in your own will, and toward judgment and the fearful punishment of Hell. Remember, God is not mistaken; it will do no good to argue with Him. A loving God urges you, "Prepare to meet thy God!"

Think what it would mean to be lost. Count the cost! Lost!! Without hope! Don't wait for a more convenient time. Come to God now. "Seek ye the Lord while He may be found."

\* \* \* \*

This may be your first real introduction to God's plan of salvation. On the other hand you may be one of the many professing Christians to whom the Lord will speak those fateful words, "I never knew you." You never were really born again. You may have believed—but as you now analyze your belief you realize that it has been really only mental, and not from the heart, as it *must* be. "With the *heart* man believeth unto righteousness." If what you have called being a Christian has not included surrender to God and a changed life, you are still in your sins —and lost! Don't compare yourself with others who claim to be Christians. Your only safe guide is the Word of God!

You are at the point of decision, friend. You cannot be neutral in this matter. As you

*Page Twenty-eight*

lay this booklet down you will do one of two things: You will either sincerely surrender your heart to God and receive His forgiveness, or, you will continue in your self-willed living and toward the judgment which will surely follow. Your decision now may be your last. *Your eternal destiny is at stake!* ...A wrong decision here may influence your family, and loved ones and friends, and drag them with you into the same chaos toward which you have decided to continue, while a decision for God may lead them all to surrender to God and receive forgiveness and eternal life through Jesus Christ. You'll never regret such a decision. You'll thank God for it throughout eternity.

\* \* \* \*

The Devil is a real being, and he will give you every reason possible why you can safely put this decision off until later. He will tell you that there is still plenty of time.

Don't let the Devil fool you! The issue is too great! The stakes are too high! Also, the game of sin is *fixed* and you *cannot* win. The pleasures of sin and the temporary winnings only serve as the "come on" which gets you more deeply involved. You can win by leaving the game NOW, no matter how deeply you are involved. The Devil knows that if he can get you to put off surrendering to God now that it will be comparatively easy for him to get you to put it off tomorrow,

*Page Twenty-nine*

and the next day and the next—until it's too late!

Pray for God's help in this time of decision! This is a matter of life or death, of wondrous eternal joy or hopeless doom. This could be God's *last call to you.* **You know the way**—you have no reason to expect further mercy from God. If you decide to continue a little longer in your sin, God may decide you've had your last chance!

Talk it over with our heavenly Father, while He is willing and waiting to receive you as His very own. Surrender your heart in love and obedience to Him NOW.

"Seek ye the Lord while He may be found. Call ye upon Him while He is near."

Will you sincerely make the following prayer to God *your* prayer?

**"Lord be merciful to me—a lost sinner! Forgive me Lord! My only hope is placed in Jesus Christ who died for me. Possess my heart, and reign there supreme. Lead me by your Holy Spirit that I may know your will in all things. My Lord! My Savior! My God!"**

My name ..............................

Date ................................

If the above is YOUR prayer, do this. Write this prayer on a sheet of paper in your own handwriting, and sign your name, and

*Page Thirty*

date. As you write, say the words in your heart to God. Make it your very own prayer, from the bottom of your heart. Keep that paper forever! It will be a reminder to you of the day you turned to Jesus—from sin and God's punishment, to God's forgiveness and everlasting life.

And then, as soon as possible, tell somebody the good news that you have truly believed in Jesus Christ and that you have received Him as your Lord and Savior. "If thou shalt confess with thy mouth the Lord Jesus, and shalt believe in thine heart that God hath raised Him from the dead, THOU SHALT BE SAVED. For with the heart man believeth UNTO RIGHTEOUSNESS; and with the mouth confession is made UNTO SALVATION. For the scripture saith, Whosoever believeth on Him shall not be ashamed." Romans 10:9-11.

If He is truly your Lord you will not be ashamed to stand up and be counted on His side, by speaking up for Him.

Don't fail here. Confessing Christ to others by baptism and by the words of your mouth are evidences to God of your sincerity. Your changed life will be the other evidence.

Not all your friends will appreciate your testimony, but some will. You may lose some of your old friends, because there are those who will refuse to go God's way, and you

*Page Thirty-one*

cannot continue to go with them in their way. But God will give you many wonderful new friends to replace those you lose.

Don't wait until you are better able to testify for Christ. You learn by doing. God will understand any present lack of ability or knowledge on your part—and your friends need your witness now. Countless numbers have never been shown the real truth. Tell them of Christ in the best way you know how.

And maybe you can share the message of this booklet with them. Don't fail them! And don't fail your Lord.

## IMPORTANT INSTRUCTIONS

Just this further word for you when you have made your peace with God—There is much that God wants every Christian to know, both concerning this life and that which is beyond. This important knowledge is obtained through reading the Bible and through fellowship with God in prayer.

It's best for a new Christian to read the New Testament first. Start with the book of Matthew, chapter one, verse 18.

\* \* \* \*

We would suggest that you read this message through again. The profound truths presented here cannot be fully digested in one reading. And this time, ask God to be with you as you read.

**US Army Huey Helicopter that Mom & Pop flew in at times**

# About the Author

Nora Kincaid Pinter was born in a log cabin on the shores of Lake Osoyoos near the Canadian border in the state of Washington. When she was about two years old, the family, Wade and Ruth Kincaid and her two older siblings, Esther and Wade Jr., moved to a small farming community in Eastern Washington. Her youngest sibling Nancy Kay was added to the family. There her father started a church known as the Mission Church. Her parents believed in and trusted God for every aspect of their lives. They were very strict disciplinarians but loving and wanting God's very best for their children. Nora rebelled against this strictness, but God in his mercy and prayers of her parents found her way back to a life of living for and trusting God. God's grace and mercy have been witnessed in her own family so many times. As she most recently was reminded of was a car-train accident. She and her husband and four children were going to a church potluck dinner. It was dark and raining and as they approached a curve and railroad tracks, they noticed there was a train sitting on the tracks, no lights, and no warning. The reason they were even able to see there was a train was because of the cars that stopped on the other side of the track, and their lights were shining through the wheels of the train. Her husband hit the brakes and the car skidded and hit the train car, broke the windshield, and miraculously the car stopped. It was only God's protection that kept them from being decapitated. So many times over the past sixty-five years, they have seen God's marvelous love at work.

She lives in Spokane, Washington, with Jim, her husband of sixty-five years. They are blessed with four children, eleven grandsons, and thirteen great-grandchildren.

CPSIA information can be obtained
at www.ICGtesting.com
Printed in the USA
BVHW061606210423
662798BV00024B/874